ROCK ARRANGEMENT

CMUP Literary Translation

Nicky Agate and Jake Grefenstette, Series Editors

Also by Yan An

A Naturalist's Manor, translated by Chen Du and Xisheng Chen

Middle-Aged Man's Self-Portrait, translated by Chen Du and Xisheng Chen

ROCK ARRANGEMENT

POEMS BY

YAN AN

TRANSLATED BY

CHEN DU & XISHENG CHEN

CARNEGIE MELLON UNIVERSITY PRESS

PITTSBURGH 2026

Book design by Connie Amoroso

Library of Congress Control Number 2026937115
ISBN 978-0-88748-745-3
Original Chinese copyright © 2013 by Yan An
English translation copyright © 2026 by Chen Du and Xisheng Chen
All rights reserved
Printed and bound in the United States of America

10 9 8 7 6 5 4 3 2 1

Contents

I NORTHERN WRITER

II WHALES AND TERRITORY

III A COORDINATOR'S CANYON

IV PLANE AND SNOW

V MOUNTAIN ALWAYS WORSHIPPED BY ME

VI ROCK ARRANGEMENT

I
NORTHERN WRITER

Northern Writer

I will write in the way *The Classic of Mountains and Seas* was written
About the plummeting of a mountain as if toward an abyss
With a tower its tapering spire as a perch for many birds
And its original dove gray color I will write about
The quietude and doldrums grimmer than winter
About the bird droppings dust star shards
On the spire all cleaned once every five years
By a lonesome missionary and people designated by him

I will even write about the entire North
After the surrounding mountains are flattened
After the high-rises and gigantic chimneys
Become more magnificent than the mountains
After one river three rivers and nine rivers
Are lodged in the bowels of the city like sewers

I will write about the entire North's plummeting
As if toward an abyss and its plummeting flight tightly tied up
With its extensive yet slightly languid wings and love
The flight disregarding life and death
As desperate as plummeting

Those Northern Blue Lakes

Only by traversing thousands of miles of yellow sands
And thousands of mountain ranges
Can one see those blue lakes
Where every day stars ignite lights
To wait for the curtain of night to fall

The rocks of unknown origin belonging only to the North
Are scattered along the shore like constellations
Like star debris they wait for the stars in the lakes to illuminate
Then they all will stealthily weep for a while without any explanation
Face-to-face with loss   just like long-lost relatives

I believe the lakes too are awaiting my arrival
Not by aircraft   but by foot alone
Not at a young age   but after walking a lifetime
When I am almost too old to walk but dodder

The lights kindled by the stars in the northern blue lakes are so lonesome
And so are those constellation-like giant boulders on the shore
They have always been waiting for my arrival
Waiting for my entry into my twilight years
When I can go nowhere   but light up together
The lamps on the shore and the stars having slumbered for a long time
On the hearts of the massive boulders

Black Iron and Dark Cloud

A piece of black iron will be like a dark cloud
Only in the northern wilderness
And only when the constellations in the night sky fade in
And gradually shroud everything with their dim light
Can you feel the piece of black iron with the same glimmers
Like a seed deposited in time   as if the firmament
Had deposited its once-dejected soul in a corner of the earth
To slowly await those advancing for a harvest

A dark cloud will be like a piece of black iron
Only in the northern wilderness
And only when its furry fuzzy antennae
Are drenched in the gloomy light of the constellations
Can you feel its dark-iron-like fullness and freedom
It doesn't need any harvest
Just like the heart of a silent trekker on the earth
Who doesn't need any harvest   except the constellations
The dim light of a piece of black iron
The furry fuzzy comfort of a flowery dark cloud
And walking alone

A piece of black iron and a dark cloud
Respectively in and above the northern wilderness
Under the gloomy light of the constellations
Are simultaneously sipping the heaviness and lightness
Only weighable by the glimmers of the constellations

A Flyable Kid

A flyable kid
Is soaring with a black plane with black iron wings
And a big white bird with giant angelic sails

The black plane is sailing toward the northern capital airport
While the giant white bird is winging southward   southward
Toward the desolate and uninhabited Pacific Ocean

However the flyable kid
Has no wings just like an aircraft
His flight invisible to any navigator
With no place to land
Speedier and speedier like a meteorite
Is producing gusts of cold smoke
(But not hot incinerated air)

The flyable kid
Is infatuated with the flight gradually climaxing like a game
His flight is unknown to anyone
The place he is about to land
(A fatal landing   one even without
Enough time for a shriek)

Is an uncharted place
More remote and desolate than the innermost heart

Over-Blustery Gale

A gale has damaged a train
Zooming forward like a giant python in the northern wilderness
And darkened the snow-white clouds above the Pacific
As well as the languid face of the sun
Dozing off amidst the icy snow in the center of a warm convection flow
A livid brazen face just like an outdated white radish

The dark face of the sun in the gale
Has scared a black plane silly
High above the Pacific Ocean
And has mercilessly and ruthlessly broken
The giant wings of a white swan and a big plane
The desperate swan having no time to mourn
And the gigantic plane with broken wings
Chase each other and plunge together into the Pacific
In the over-blustery gale

The over-blustery gale
Has also blown down a massive boulder on a lonesome island
Cut open the breast of a colossal whale in an anonymous trench
Leaping above the sea once in a while
And then thrown its soft limp body
Like folding a piece of unclaimed clothing
Gently into
The Pacific Ocean
With an appetite nothing can sate
Not even meteorites

The Extremity of the Earth

At the extremity of the earth there are mists
The shadow of a boy
Chased by a lizard in the swelter
And an ant tempted by the reek of blood
From dawn to dusk
Thus leading some other ants
To hurry off to another place

I witness them   in a desert not far
Traverse a grove of blooming peaches and green willows
As well as an expanse of low-lying marshy grassland
And disappear as if in a rush
Together with some mysterious mists
On a path toward the extremity of the earth

I am going to collect the mists
The bones of goats   horses   camels
As white as the mists   gnawed and left over by wolves
And the skeletons of anonymous victims
As well as the scrap iron   paint buckets
Worn-out scaffold-like lathes
And cast iron scraps piled up everywhere as if in martyrdom
In abandoned factories

Onlooker

The suspicious odyssey of an onlooker
Wearing a broad-brimmed straw hat in the northern summer
Is reaching its climax—sometimes punctuated by peaks
Otherwise concealed by a gloomy canyon—
And is obviously slowing down
While gradually approaching a desert

A prairie on one side and sandy land on the other
The views bewilder him who also witnesses
A river wagging its tail and a startled lizard
Too desperate to choose its path
Travel together   hurriedly vanishing into the distance

It is when a truck faster than the river rushes by
That I behold the onlooker   his bewilderment
Unconcealable by the shadow under his broad-brimmed straw hat
And his abruptly stopped journey
With an apex mingled with slight abjection

Lone River

I will begin my writing with the smallest river
A rivulet in a desert

Living on the riverside of the creek in the desert
Are lizards and a ladybug family
All with temporal yet bewildering flights
And seemingly casual life with game-like courtship and mating
Red rocks   gunmetal-gray rocks   steel-blue rocks
And even black rocks
Seem to slumber inside time
Like a game half-played by a child
The rivulet   in the dream of an unkempt child
In the varicolored dream of the heap of rocks
Carelessly and recklessly traverses the border

The rivulet in the desert
Is so translucent that its sand grains as sober as crystals
Remain indifferent to the boundless and indistinct grassland
With sand dunes gently rolling with a zephyr
To the mire and disheveled weeds piled up on the riverbed
And to the repeated enveloping and wavering crossing
Of the dark umbra of a red-beaked crow flying over the sky

The rivulet in the desert
Remains nonchalant to an outlander overlooking while resting
Under the sporadic umbrage of an unexpected tree on a hill afar
And to the melancholy flickering and glooming alternatively
In the depths of his eyes
Just like fire sparks

A Boy's Trek

A boy is chasing his own shadow from behind
In the wilderness
On a mountain summit
And while racing on the other bank after hopping over a great river
With his phantom ingenuous sincerity

He drums the water while yapping and growling toward the sun
On the shore of a lake with numerous migrant birds killed by thirst
The sun-scorched lake is as red as fire
The boy is full of the water as if full of flames
He turns away and dashes more crazily
To pursue the shadow
Which is tortured by flames in the dark
Which tries to extricate itself with a temptation for the yonder
Which he attempts to stop perpetually
After a deadly strike with the large pile of glazed fireballs
He wants to disgorge from his stomach
And which he is going to merge his entire body into
By lowering his body's inclination further and further

I am the man dreaming of the boy chasing his shadow from behind
Or maybe the very man enticed by his own shadow
I am indeed the boy dashing after his own shadow
I aspire to trek farther and farther

My Hometown Is to the North of the Qin Mountains

People of the world all know   to the north of the Qin Mountains
(With many things always hidden very deeply)
Lies my hometown
Where the moon over the hill is tinted with a blush
As if it had just cried   a river is inside grasslands
Deity and Buddhist statues in stone shrines
Smoked by burning incense
Have a swarthy look with a red shine
Just like Father's reddish face glimmering with some
Repressed yet warm luster in his blackish stubble
After being repeatedly cleansed by life and dust

People of the world all know my hometown
However they don't know   tied down by small children
While roving in another place all these years
I always love to keep silent in the darkness
(A character brought from my hometown)

In the dark   whenever recalling that Father
Out of his senses   was wailing alone on the hill like a wolf
With his aged red face covered in tears
After having slaughtered an old ox by the river
"I can only run farther and farther   whereas no matter how far I run
My heart is pent up with those inescapable wails"
That continue to chase after the psychic livestock
In those years   the miserable state of mind
Of a countryman having seen the truth
My father and I   were always too ashamed to speak up

People of the world all know   in my hometown
The specters of livestock torture life longer than human souls
Destitution is a misunderstanding existent since ancient times
Nurtured on its trees are no bird chirps and whirrs
But leaves plummeting downward in autumn
Cultivated in its rivers are no fish   except frogs' croaks
Which on a moonlit night
Can pierce through the exuberant grass in the center of the river
Sometimes whispering and muttering like Father
Other times weeping and sobbing like a little baby
Rendering the nocturnal scenery
More quiet and poignantly beautiful

People of the world all know   in my hometown
The village where Father and Mother expected to be interred
Nowadays appears to be emptier
One winter when I returned
It was already the day when my father was consigned to the grave
Snow was like white clothes wrapping tightly
The bodies of the bereaved kin as stiff as wooden sticks
The wails were as meandering and rigid as the frozen river

People of the world all know   to the north of the Qin Mountains
Lie my hometown and the hometown of many other people
None of them knows that   there are
Fewer and fewer people each passing day
With luxuriant grass and the solitary croaks of frogs

South North

Living in the North   prickled with mountains
As well as many spacious places
I am actually more used to surveying tiny things
With my stocky compact body
In a lower place   in various valleys and dales

Those more minute than I are mole crickets ants   some rats
That crisscross the humble underground
Producing sounds penetrating into another world
Those calmer yet more timid than I are wild beasts
That egress and ingress the mountain woods
Chased by poachers   and on a moonless windy night
Get lost occasionally in the wilderness

There are times when I scale the mountains   look high up
Stray in the wilderness just like a wind
And look afar into the place where mists rise
Nevertheless I will not think highly of this universe
Nor will I get inextricably immersed in bewilderment

Staying in the North all year   I witness eye-openers everywhere
When the North-loving migrant birds return again
And bring tidings of the South   where
Heavy rainstorms have caused disastrous floods this summer
And many people have perished in the horrid heat

My valleys and I   even the entire North
Can't help but fall into prolonged quietude
Thinking of many of the inherently low southern places

Our hearts mourning   start to plummet heavily
Toward the South

And like a bird whose heart ruptures abruptly
Or a never-weighted steelyard weight
Are descending from the celestial arc
Speedily

Mu Us Desert, Encountering a Herder Too Old to Have Consciousness

Paler than the belly of a dead fish
And more pallid than salt and alkali
The desert now is dwelling in his ears
In his eyes
In his sweat pores and hair follicles
And in his throat

From his aged flesh drained by the sun
No more grease or moisture can be squeezed out
His set of old coatrack-like bones
Can no longer grandly prop up the skin
Draping like a heap of rags

Before he tells me anything
He starts to cough aloud
With the sound piercing into
His lungs having atrophied to the smallest size
And not diggable even by a lancet

The old man standing against the wind
Later coughs out a mere slight teardrop
Too tiny to moisten
A gunk at the corner of an eye
In a trance tears diffuse inside me
Like well water

Sleeping with a Mirror

A snow-white swan
(Or maybe just a similar whitish thing)
With its somewhat unreal whiteness
In an autumn heavenly lake
A place farther than Xinjiang
Is sleeping with a mirror

A massive curved boulder with black moss
And a large heap of shining white bird droppings
On a precipitous cliff above a great river
In the ancient wind   under the wings
Of a bird attempting to determine its flight gesture
Is sleeping with time

A snake having sloughed off its white skin in a jungle
(All these exist only in imagination)
Fruitlessly chased a hungry tiger
Lost its way back to its pit
And hence fled helter-skelter out of fright
Needs to hasten to the moorland before night falls
To sleep with gloomy clouds and the moon

My father and his gray hair
As well as his white bones under his dark skin
All glitter-glistening with chilling white shimmers
With nowhere to rest
And all with certain indescribable melancholy
In the homeland's dreams and mine tonight
Are sleeping with the northern mountains

Mountain in My Childhood

First a precipice with massive towering boulders
And small cypresses draping invertedly
Then a stretch of mountainside with no visible end
Finally a magnificent yet lonesome tree on the mountaintop
With wailing birds accompanied by the bright moon
On a late summer night

I always scaled the mountain alone   from ages eight to ten
On my own I clambered up the precipice
And threaded my way through the wimpled wheat
Shrouding the entire hillside
The wheat grew taller than I   so I could never overlook
The mountaintop merging into the sky or the tree atop

A few times I completely strayed
Which seemed like a setup by a ghost
The rustles and susurrations of the wheatland in the blustering wind
Frightened me further and further
My outcries could be heard by no one   nor could my weeps
My desperation rendered me tightly embracing a wheat stalk
Dejectedly sitting down and gradually dozing into slumberland
In the middle of the wheat field

Actually I just wanted to see on the mountaintop
How many species of birds were indeed dwelling on the tree
And to count how many nests were actually built in the canopy

Wild Kid

In order to travel farther and farther with each passing day
A wild kid chooses to climb a train for a ride in spring
Crisscross the airport in winter
And to inquire about an old pirate having disappeared for years
And his oceanic mask fully decorated with monster patterns
On the pier toward the waters with a controversial orientation
In an attempt to sail afar on the ocean in summer

The wild kid   many times inevitably unkempt and unwashed
Bouncing and bustling about like a busy bee
Comprehends very well many things must be searched for in the yonder

More often   in some places called a strange land
He is continuously driven out by people from the train station
Or constantly stranded at the airport for national ID card issues
The smoke swirling around the cigarettes
Covers up again and again those seemingly familiar faces

Completely melancholy he beholds them
Gradually seeing through and outguessing them
Just as he once penetrated a few lice
Parasitizing deep hair and linen-lined clothing
And a few small lead coins as evasive as paupers
In a canvas backpack corroded by grease

Now ahead of time he even beholds a future seashore
Or open land far from the ocean and signs of human habitation
Where he is snuffing out lice
When he is content with it
He will race toward afar without any restraint

A Man Is Leaving the North

A plane and its trail of black smoke over the Qin Mountains
Are the masks of the North and the celestial dome
A crow and its hesitant flight   are the masks
Of a summer high noon   with an unknown outcome

A man   is trekking uneasily in the northern wilderness
Being far off   sometimes he appears as tiny as an ant
He is practicing Chinese Mandarin on his own
Attempting to disguise himself before leaving his homeland
For a train station in winter and an airport in summer
As the earth's mask about to journey to a remote land

The man about to leave the North
Is preparing never to return again
Yet unexpectedly finds that   a lone chimney in the moors
With a wisp of languid and listless smoke above it
Seems like a doomsday fish nosediving in the ocean
And abruptly concealing itself in the depths
As if it were mourning the nameless summer
And ninety-nine nameless masks about to be exhibited
In a summer meeting held on pine branches

In the nameless summer   with layers of masks
And the man about to leave the North
Even a plane and an entire train cannot carry
His shadow and the heaviness
As anonymous as a mask   yet faint and blurred
In his innermost heart

Qinghai Province: Snow in My Childhood

Beautiful snow was falling in my childhood
When I was in foster care in Xining City
Oh my frail destitute childhood
Nice snow was whistling in a northern gale
Zigzagging down in cold and rigid Qinghai Province
The wonderful yet grayish snow
Was rushing down from a magnificent mountain
Together with dark hill-like clouds
Onto the dampness that a little boy tried to hide
Behind his eyes and puerile cheeks
After having wept for a while for nostalgia
Behind the backs of other people

Calamity of Pearls

There are many things on Earth from outer space
Such as pearls   ever since my childhood
I have been determined to acquire some
Thereby I too became a man receiving the call of destiny
Before adulthood and then escaping my hometown
As if fleeing a calamity

My grandpa knew I was a man journeying afar for pearls
When he went to heaven   I was in Tibet
On a mountain higher than his soul
For the first time I craned my neck to overlook my hometown
For the first time I cried my heart out empty-handed
My father knew I was a man looking for pearls
In his dreams he could repeatedly see me
Hold pearls in my hands with my head broken and bleeding
Therefore he broke out in a cold sweat every day
Haunted by a nightmare every night

Later I knew   none of the people in our village
Having brought back pearls from the wild
Had come to a good end: some inexplicably became insane
Galloping wildly along the mountain ridges
Like a mountain ghost for a lifetime
Some ignored the presence of all the other people
Tirelessly talking false nonsense to the sky day and night
Others had disappeared for many years   but sudden news
Came that their corpses had lain on the streets of strange lands

Actually I have always been changing myself
For example not long ago I finally returned to my village home

To visit my father much older than my grandpa from my memory
But only to find that he still cherished an undying unchangeable heart
Just before parting he kept admonishing me:
"There are many pearls in the city; if you like them you can see more
However in no case should you bring one back home
A nice pearl scorches the hand and even kills!"
Even though somewhat absent-minded
I still promised to him like a docile child
While agreeing with him
I was still the man walking outward
The man embracing in his bosom dust and wildness
The man having failed in his years of searching for pearls
The man maneuvered by things from outer space

Nevertheless I have memorized the moment
The moment when the village was shrouded in vast hazy twilight
When my father and the other people seeing me off
Gradually faded into the tenebrosity
When I too merged little by little into the darkness
All of a sudden I lost control
Upheld my empty hands in the dark for nothing
And couldn't help bursting into hot tears

Doll with a Straw Headscarf

He likes a crow's slant yet gradually approaching flight
And its prophesying quietude
Or chattering noise containing more signs than a prophecy
After it skims over him

Nevertheless his prediction is empty empty in spring
Empty in summer empty in winter as well
Just like the empty chunks of ice and bird nests on power lines
After a blizzard extensively buffeted and tossed by a northern gale
Just like the empty face as white as a shroud
Of a eunuch with subdued deficient fire
Just like the empty winter wilderness
Left by the person having appreciated the autumn
Together with him and then returned home

The doll with a straw headscarf
Has frolicked too much with the crow when the crow
Rushes to another place for another chant
He stands alone lacerated gradually by a gale
Thus exposing little by little the hollowness inside his body
The emptiness represented by a mat of shabby straws in his heart
And the desolate and derelict emptiness of the entire hills and dales
Stressed by his emptiness

Night Train

Black rails traverse the vast expanse of the white North
Like two dejected human beings
And stretch into the northern night's
Tenebrosity not having been serene since last year
The kind of darkness of the tottering boulders
Having been completely removed from cliffs by sappers

People leaving the North under the cover of late night
With an empty yet weary countenance
Are clinging close to the windows
As if having fallen into memories
They and the lights entrapped in the coaches
Are gazing at each other

They just want to look at a place one last time
(Though this is by no means their only objective)
A village with no signs of human habitation
One confined to empty houses and deserted courtyards

One abruptly brightened up by the night train
Rushing out of a tunnel
And then speedily left behind

A Story of Return to Home Village

Upon seeing my face Mother cried
So hard as to have fainted a few times
While Father   with his silence for days running
Reminded me that
Many people I knew had gone
Many people unknown to me had moved elsewhere
So I could spare much of the ritual of visiting
In such an empty village deserted by old acquaintances

The mountain of my childhood memory
Nowadays has become a crisscross network of roads
Filled with the roar of engines and machines
Only when night fell did I realize
The majestic tree on the hilltop was gone as well
Replaced by a mightier and taller steel headframe
Standing aloft with searchlights
Raking an area with a ten-kilometer radius
The earth afar was no longer indistinct
And I didn't need to overlook it from a high place

I wanted to take my parents with me   however
They had already arranged a graveyard
"The time to return has been determined
There is no need to journey afar
No road is farther than the path of life and death
We are like candles burned out at the ends
Just start out and bon voyage"

The day I left   Mother stopped weeping
Even the face of silent Father beamed with delight

Wafting down from the mountain were cries like cattle howls
Allegedly they were from Second Uncle
Of the few households remaining in the village
His only son trafficked crude oil with PP sacks and tractors
And died after falling from the cliff at night three years ago
Becoming a heap of crumbled flesh in a pile of iron scraps

I paused for a long time
Somewhat hesitant yet inexplicably impulsive
The mountain of my childhood memory
With a large portion destroyed by dynamites
The cliff appearing more dangerous due to dilapidation
Second Uncle wailing while squatting like a black dog
The last few small tortuous yet lonesome cypresses on the precipice
Father and Mother quietly seeing me off on the hillside

I couldn't turn around to overlook them one last time
As if my throat were suddenly stuck with
A pile of unswallowable ice cubes
With a fit of light dizziness
I instantly fell into sorrowfulness and couldn't help myself
For a long long time

Outlanders

Outlanders came to my hometown in the North

Those outlanders   with non-native accents
And nonlocal faces   were as chubby as ducks
As stupid as pigs   yet fond of
Scaling mighty mountains just like me

They brought tidings to the entire village
A road would be built to the mountain
The cliff with massive boulders would be blasted
The wimpled wheat would be driven to the slopes of another mountain
Just that the tree on the mountaintop was somewhat miraculous
A disposal project was under study

Many times I tailed them
Beheld them screaming while climbing up at the risk of their lives
Quietly counted from their behind those buttocks
Big or small   of either a male or a female
And witnessed how they wiggle-waggled frightenedly
With slight gloat   short of hatred

This seems to be out of the norm
For many years   I seemed to have disappeared
For many years   I seemed to have never existed
For many years   I seemed to have been deceased
I have left my hometown
And too become an outlander

Balloon and Emptiness

Earth is like an unexpected balloon
With a solid inside and an empty outside
Floating in the endless emptiness

Earth wafting in the boundless emptiness like a balloon
With a heavy head   heavy wings   a heavy heart
Has so easily bumped a plane down like blowing off dust
Smashed an eagle
And even tossed an inadvertently toppled hill
Into the ocean like dumping trash
And thereby returned the emptiness
They once occupied pointlessly
To the infinite hollowness
Which only the universe can match

Thus rendering itself wafting like a balloon
In the limitless emptiness
A shape as sensitive yet solid as a heart
And the truth of the entire emptiness
Verifiable by a balloon
Harder to rupture than a heart yet explodable
By excessive internal emptiness

II

WHALES AND TERRITORY

Territory

From Helan Mountains to Qin Mountains
(Oh two miraculous mountains keeping out
The northern gales and southern rains)
From one massive boulder to another
Across a roaring river
And several quiet yet somewhat bizarre rivers
Deserts   marshy grasslands   jungles
The height of a soaring bird   of an eagle
And the depth of a fish   of a marmot   of an earthworm
It is my territory

Horses' territory

The territory where my ancestors and their bones
Rest like stones abandoned and scattered everywhere
Where legends and fairy tales
Thrive with an endless circle of life
Just like wild grass and flowers

I know this undulant earth's   this territory's
Once cherished self-esteem
Is the gray quivering bristles and manes
As sharp as daggers   of a pack of dashing wolves
I know the speed
With which a lake is omitted from history by a desert
And with which a stray dove escapes into the firmament
It has been accustomed to the azure blue of the lake
As well as the freshness of freshwater fish
Nevertheless it hasn't adapted to
The azure blue of the celestial arc

The sad and shrill northwestern gales
And the unbearably feeble flight
With all its energy depleted

Railroad tracks as close and dense as ribs
National highways like layers after layers of bandages
Wrapping a seriously injured person
Petroleum towers growling and bellowing like giant monsters
With searchlights able to rend the entire universe

As to how some odd birds and their nests
Mysteriously disappeared
How a tomb-robbing gang with cast-iron Luoyang shovels
Shimmering gloomily yet ruthlessly in a lonesome valley
Was raided by a swarm of cops
Had their deaths co-buried forever with underground white bones
And thereby disappeared without a trace

Today I am the man on horseback in quest of secrets
The man driven to track them down
The man digging thoroughly in the local area
As if trespassing on a strange land
In an attempt to collect information

Tunnel Warfare

I always want to build a subterranean tunnel
Which my rivals and all the antitheses in the universe
Couldn't make heads or tails of it will by no means
Be like a mole very impetuously concealing
Its timidity at the mere rustle of leaves in the wind
Or be like an earthworm disliking the tenebrosity
In the world for not being fierce enough
Thereby burrowing through the underground
To look for a darker inkiness and then dwelling inside
Or be like the underground tunnels in the Qin Mountains
Having perforated the belly of a deity
Tormented by spacious pitch-dark mortification
And vacuously and frustratedly waiting for their retribution

The subterranean tunnel I always want to build
Has been designed in my heart for many years
Located at the extremities of all cardinal directions
And a location without any address
It is by no means abstract instead very concrete
For example it would be right on a precipice
In its leisure time a kind of bird
Never heard of before would fly over
Dwell for a period of time while taking advantage
Of the occasion to reproduce and parent
If the tunnel were in a canyon the wild beasts having vanished
In legends would come back crisscross it
And then disappear without leaving any traceable vestige

For another example if a person is fortunate enough to live there
They could only light the place with candles

And breathe the fragrance and scents of plants
With their cell phone signal automatically vanished
For another instance only I would be familiar with the path to it
The stalkers having been thrown off by me one by one
At crucial moments   would abruptly stop
At a crossroad   looking right and left
At their wits' end   like blind men

I have always been building such a tunnel
Maybe when it's finished it won't come in handy
Or maybe one day   actually for no rhyme or reason
I would just want to play the hide-and-seek game with myself
I would go there
To hide away

Settling

Everything you see in the world   has been settled
Just as a mountain with the pet name Lonesome
Has settled two rivers   with one on each side
And has arranged all the fish and Trionyx sinensis
In both rivers to be either fat or thin
And an aquatic species different from fish and Trionyx sinensis
To be disturbingly and disquietingly hideous
What kinds of birds should wing in the celestial dome
What kinds of foxes and rats should scurry in the mountains
A village on an inlet   an old boat berthed at an old ferry
All of these have been secured

The world you behold   as if it had been fixed up
And the great thick plains   will dawn on you one day
If you live at very low altitude   the weather
Will inevitably be somewhat abnormal and adverse
In addition you are not alone in this world
The sewer drain is clogged every day with many rivers
As the origin   as to farther places it's a different thing
A lot of mud and filth there can only be taken away
By thunder   lightning   tempests

The world you witness   being installed again and again
Now unhinges your mind   you must get situated
The deceased people floating downstream
Along the great raging river   the excessive deposits
On the riverbed   big fish and old Trionyx sinensis
Stinky in less than two days   and tough boulders
Stronger and more durable than steel and iron

In the world you observe   everyone else is settling down
So you should be settled as well   though it's not easy
You must   in the depths of jealousy and narrow-mindedness
Scrape off your scales   as if scaling a live fish
Or skinning and eating yourself alive
And butcher yourself   as if slaughtering a person
From another dynasty   or carving up a fish

Then   time flies and flashes by
Even when facing imminent disaster or death
You are still a trekker with a mind unhinged
On the road   in order to accommodate yourself
As well as the darkness as suspect as
The subterranean tunnels inside the universe
You hasten to another place

After Abrupt Disappearance of a Lake

All local deserts
Were originally under an azure-green lake
Under the bellies of fish
Under the decayed hulls of boats of old boatmen

Like the lungs of the entire nation being furtively eroded
The exposed sandy land after the abrupt disappearance of the lake
Is catastrophically sprawling into neighboring regions
The trees are splayed on the ground like mandarin pancakes
The grass is following suit
And so are the shrubs   and the worms having lost their shelters
By leading a flock of varicolored birds to fly away

Even a traveler having arrived by chance
Is following suit in slumberland
He has dreamed of: when some other lakes successively perish
Kua Fu having been in sopor all day and every day[1]
In the desert will eventually awaken   stretching his
Body and limbs   disgorging in whole ten suns
Having been swallowed by him for ten millennia
As if puking up pearls   and the heart like a tough stone
In the wilderness uncrushable even if compressed
Repeatedly by the ten suns

Whilst his eyes having spouted flames once will spew out
In regret   two lakes   ten giant black-backed fish

---

1. Kua Fu (夸父; pinyin: kuā fù) is a giant in Chinese mythology who wished to capture the sun.

And some kind of unheard-of singular birds
Resembling both a duck and a swan with premarital pregnancy

—"Hey! I am saying let's not discuss right now whether or not
This kind of thing can happen!"

Heavy Metal: Marilyn Manson and His Rock Portrait

His ex-wife is a stripping star
With untamed breasts planted in her body
The blue of the heavily smelly ocean
And glass blood vessels with readable gauges
The blue of a porcelain vase that can render
Roses and rosebushes forever blooming
His other ex-wife is a coal dealer
Occasionally engaging in petroleum shipping
And under the starshine arranging for popular ebony people
To bosom heavy metal   a kind of metal
Damper and damper   more and more bashful

Whereas snow   has churned up dust and rocks
On the border of dreams
Driven a bulldozer loaded with dead debris
Transformed him into an old world
And entrusted the poison suffocating the old world
To a messenger of heavy metal
Slumbering in the blue of a rose vase

(A man   cannot part with heavy metal
The world cannot forgo it either
Its serene slumber in the darkness
Its lethality at a certain level
Or its reticent sharpness)

Central Shaanxi Plain

The Central Shaanxi Plain having produced
Such a good place as Xi'an City
Is actually a basin   as mysterious as
A woman's womb   wearing layers of masks:
Emperors   imperial concubines   legends
With a countenance more rigid and thereby
More melancholy than those
Of the Terra-Cotta Warriors and Horses

The Wei River   the Jing River   the Ba River
These rivers once rendering beauties and time
Plump and velvety-skinned together
Seem to disappear nowadays without anyone
Caring about their whereabouts anymore
In the subway station like an underground palace
Newly built for a lascivious yet melancholy emperor
For hiding gold and settling his young beauties
A subway car fully loaded with drowsy passengers
Like a revenant reincarnated from an unknown dynasty
Flashes by in the lights resembling red eyes
Half asleep half awake

This is an era with sewers more important than rivers
An era with more discussions of the dome models
In subway tunnels than of the celestial dome
The Central Shaanxi Plain   a basin as mysterious as
The womb of a woman nowadays is only the bottom
Of a bowl repeatedly churned up
A basin ungauged by anyone with his body
One having been repeatedly buried and unearthed

By the golden yellow of wheat   smog
Snow granules   hidden rivers and castles stolen
One by one from all corners of the world

Place I Passed by Occasionally

It seems to be a once relatively well-worshipped temple
Or the courtyard of a man of fame
However it happened in a dynasty having died a long time ago

The dynasty existing once upon a time has vanished into thin air
A place with its owners never coming back again
And having nowadays been handed over to spiders to watch

Where even the scents of humans and ghosts will gradually dissipate
And where woods and slight murderous intentions
Live symbiotically and thrive further and further

It's certain   this place becoming barren for a long long time
Will never become   no matter how long it takes
Wolves' heaven   or fowl's paradise
At the extremity of the heavens

Heterogeneous Species

A crow and a fox
One is perching on a bough
While the other under the tree

Seeing the fox the crow loves practicing bel canto
Spotting the crow the fox wants to perform oral stunts

The crow and the fox
Heterogeneous species knowing each other's hidden truth
Compete to outsmart each other
By singing and rhetoric
And hence go to the opposite sides of the great gulf forever

Whales

The man living in a desert
Is witnessing the demise of many lakes
By his side   with his dark blue eyes
As translucent and profound as seawater
He and he   scattered to different places
By the sand dunes undulating like billows
Are people without neighbors
Taciturn for a lifetime
And when occasionally meeting together
Will talk about the ocean
They have never seen in a lifetime
The ocean's dark mass of inky blue
And whales' astonishing white
And secret prowls as of a warship

The people living in the desert
Comprehend very well the ocean and whales
And converse with each other about the accurate
Inevitable hours of an ocean and a pod of whales
And how they are resurrected and resuscitated
As if awakened   by the melody by a mermaid
On a desperate reef after their quietuses

Imagining the Life of a Spider in a Village

Woods are luxuriant
And so are weeds
And unclaimed wildflowers without fragrance
Flourishing in vast stretches and expanses
Under the boiling hot sun

In the courtyards of cave houses dilapidated one after another
Spiders are thriving
And so are cobwebs

Freely crisscrossing the cave houses under the moonlight
Are the more prosperous hares and wild ghosts
The prying of the unmotivated red eyes   highlights
The hunger of a spider in a cave house
Its wait as steady as a sure hand on the throttle
Without any illusions

A spider is destined to be hungry
The spider and its web needless of the nurture from the sun
Are in the dark   or a retreat similar to the tenebrosity
The delicately designed disk-shaped silky web
Is firmly yet extensively in control of every direction

Conveying the vigor of hunger
No longer fanciful   and nature's mystery
Only belonging to a spider

Story of Tree Planting

This year has been extraordinary
With fertile land and abundant rainfall
I will plant three trees with unsolvable mysteries
In three places untrackable even to secret agents

The first one will be planted in the anonymous bowels
Of a mountain range bristling with massive boulders
King's land with giant boulders
And all other things tirelessly gushing forth
The leader of the mountains pressing forward
And impervious to obstacles in the domain of time
My tree will love this place
The territory with grandeur roots twined freely for millennia
The eccentric-ish guidance and tolerance
Of its quiet and tranquil breadth and depth

The second one will be planted in the depths of the great plains
Where the heavy-jowled and potbellied maids of wealthy people
Were too lazy to cultivate even one inch of land
Where no water could be drawn from a well
By a pauper having inadvertently broken the copper kettle
A place deserted just like a sinner
My tree will slowly grow up there
Just like a wild child
And stand alone at the horizon like a feral kid
Who could make people flip palpating with excitement

As to the third tree   I choose the homestead
Of a giant bird and a big fish both lying at death's door
In its deeply desolate untraversed tussock grass

I have planted the tree bound to keep company
With a river and white clouds
And to spread the reputation of a river wrongfully dead
And of time   longer than ever

This year is indeed extraordinary   in the North
In the vastness   infinity   loftiness
All characteristic of the motherland
Mountains are at the height of a sailing bird
The broad view contrasts with
The diminutiveness of gray-haired rats and ants
I have planted three trees
In an unrevealed dominion like a long-lost legacy

The three trees true yet unproficient in rhetoric
Beloved stately trees
That can benumb secret agents' nerves
As if they had drunk poison
And can render devils' and great deities'
Thunderbolts and felling projects
Unable to implement any more

Are actually the trees planted in my entire
Life and death

Rivulet of Occasionality

I have been secretly enamored of a place
Neither as hard as gravel or a rock
Nor as restless   skeptical and indecisive as a sand dune
A meadow with a few dumpy-stumpy trees
Fine-grained   well-knit   but not befuddling

As if arising by chance   the thin rivulet
Drying up under the scorching sun but brimming with rainfalls
Is the river where herded horses disappear
Where a shepherd and his sheep full of river water stray
Where a lone trekker loses his sense of direction
Shortly after having a little sip of the water when crossing the river

Is the river small and discreet   seemingly humble
But being prepared every moment
For growing larger or vanishing straight

Excavator

My excavator is digging out tree roots
By an ancient house more obsolete than the old world
With specters and ghosts
Swaying sharp iron teeth like a wild beast
Ferociously biting the roots penetrating the earth
A thousand Chinese feet deep[2]
(Such massive roots   skinned piece by piece
Are also like wild beasts   grisly yet forlorn)

Oh the tree as tall as one thousand *zhang*[3]
Now seemingly made of paper   is unshowily
Tumbling down in quivers and trembles
(While its fluttering in the wind was once
Showy yet graceful and its support to birds and even clouds
Was once majestic and enigmatic)

My excavator fears no raindrops
Indefatigable   it has traveled almost everywhere
Forests   meads   rivers
And the lakes in the desert as azure blue as a mirror
It has also planned to approach the Arctic and Antarctic
Step-by-step   to excavate from the icebergs
White bears   black penguins
And the King of the Polar Whale too old to break into
A fit of coughs   all hidden deep in the ice

---

2. Chinese foot or *chi* (尺; pinyin: chǐ) is a traditional Chinese unit of length standardized in 1984 as 1/3 meter.
3. *Zhang* (丈; pinyin: zhàng) is a traditional Chinese unit of length standardized in 1984 as 3 1/3 meters.

Unlike me   my excavator has no compassion
It chases all the crocodiles
Stranded and weeping helplessly in the desert
It chases lions and elephants
Out of the woods and the tropics
Rendering them trekking aimlessly all day and every day
Mournfully and ferociously out of the horizon

Unlike me   when I caress again
Another tree one thousand *zhang* tall but dropping dead
With tears brimming in my eyes
The excavator seems to have entered an unmanned land
Like a ferocious beast gluttonous and insatiate every day
Moving on endlessly under the moonlight and starlight

Upward and Downward

Mountains are upward
(This is the reason I don't relinquish them)
Forests are upward
(That's why the earth doesn't abandon them)

Like lightning   a mottled cheetah
Is threading its way through the dimness of a forest
Its aptly appropriate hostility is upward
Forcing some little timid things
To conceal themselves more deeply
Or escape to a higher place
To refine their law of survival in lightning or icy snow
And polish their talent of running under the sun

Among the wolves' howls and tigers' roars
Even death is upward as well
Everything buried underground
Is connected to roots
There   death has liberally joined other lives
Leaving behind white bones only
Just like a soul having undergone a radical transformation
At a depth farther than before
Turning out to be clean   beautiful   radiant

The earth is upward   and so are forests and specks of dust
Even the animals and nourishments in the forests
Are upward in the form of death and mutual annihilation

The sun seems to be downward
And so is the moon   a paragon of imitators

Yet the omnipresent dust in the light
With its reticence and quietude   is so light
So close to things' intrinsic nature
That its center carrying light in the light
Is absolutely upward

The Beauty of Killing

Imitating a wild beast
I craned my neck howling
While the birds in the grove
Become more reticent than ever

Leaves shaken off like luckless birds shot by bullets
Float down from high places
Slowly and slightly hesitantly
Hide deep in tussocks of grass

Good Bird or Imaginary Bird

A good bird is prudent about flight over a city
Due to its exhaustion
And danger

A bird sailing over the top of a city
Must be sick
Dizzy and giddy
In semiconsciousness

A bird with its brain perished in the fire
Yet its wings still alive
Surely may be
A good bird

The current situation is still severe
A good bird
Should live in remote mountains
Or somewhere deeper
Like a legendary flowery cloud

A good bird would not rashly fly over a city

Beast

One or ten thousand Chinese miles a day[4]
With the speed of iron and steel it's chasing the scorching sun
With the impassive bustle of dust in a crystal clear wind
The earth continuously elevated by boulders
And a desert with plants and demised lakes at its end

Heading northward   northward   and farther
In the vastness the North is slowly ascending
Among the things continuously dwarfed: mountains
Groves   vegetation inept at concealing all its raggedness
Vehemently upturned feathers   and the flight of a crow
Depressed lower and lower by the wind
The sky and the earth have integrated more tightly than before
Like no distinction between each other
Going northward   with the speed of iron and steel
Iron and steel is traversing nihility as if the latter
Were piloting the scorching sun and the wilderness
To hasten beyond the world

At the height of a bird
Heading northward   northward   in another way
At the altitude of ten thousand meters
Where only a compass has directions   whilst the world
Has none
The aircraft is wobbling its steel skeleton
From one point to another
With a clumsy flight   bound to have

4. Chinese mile or *li* (里; pinyin: lǐ) is a traditional Chinese unit of distance standardized in 1984 as half of a kilometer (500 meters).

A terribly rough time caused by the smog
Merging into one with the sky   in its vastness
At a higher place   at the extremities of the celestial arc
Impassive clouds are waiting for you to chase
And so is the emptiness

Heading northward   whilst once waking up
I will be destined to descend
The world is a beast   and so am I
With a stark naked golden-yellow back
Having swallowed the raging fire of the world
I flash by toward the remote North

Man in a Black Bear Skin

The mountains in this region were once covered by woods
Housing bizarre trees   birds   beasts
But never bears

A man in a black bear skin
Comes down at high noon from remote mountains
And then at the edge of the city
In the remaining umbra of accumulated snow
Lingers   unwinds   and from time to time
Scratches an itch mimicking a bear
His indifferent yet imprudent countenance
As well as his black bear skin
Has attracted a lot of blank gazes
And an increasing surge   wave after wave
Of suspicion and unease
From the entire city with many snobs

The man in the black bear skin
With his dazzling pitch-blackness
And his clumsy behavior as of a black bear
Actually has shown from the very beginning
Multiple signs of attempting to change his whereabouts
But shilly-shallying
Or seems to be racking his brain to prepare
Another tactic as calm as a black bear skin
After the frustration of an agreement

Maybe he is waiting for dusk
When night falls as dark as a black bear skin
With heavy tenebrosity   increasingly scarce pedestrians

And hunter-like cops and city inspectors
Relaxing their vigilance

Tonight he will tap into the city
Just like a scheming and calculating spy
To lurk in the place
Where he has planned to go

Tiger

In the distance of summer a tiger
Sometimes paces in a leisurely manner
Other times seems severely infuriated
Zooming toward a farther place
With dread and roars or a deep sigh

In the distance of summer the tiger
Tormented by the scorching weather
So hard as to be off its rocker
Is malevolently spying on
In a direction driven by its languor and terror
The demise of an antelope approaching putrefaction
And the grains of grass not yet fully mature
Bumped down by winds and layers of flies

There is nowhere to hide
The intent of the boy
To ask the tiger for its hide
Who is hewing down woods
In the distant wasteland of summer
(Just like his innate melancholy
Revealed with no reservation by his eyes
As keen as those of an eagle)
He is experiencing summer's blatant decay
And the pain concealed under the tabby tiger's fur
Drawing near him step-by-step

Coffee-Hawking Outlander

A coffee-hawking outlander just came to our city last year
Carrying a large bamboo basket containing similar bamboo baskets
And a bag holding bags and suspicious bottles and jars
Judged by his appearance as blackish red and unfathomable as coffee
He must be from a tropical countryside or may even come from
An isolated island in the tropical ocean farther than fog

Just like a lonely islet
(As proven by the certain temperament displayed on his forehead)
The coffee-hawking outlander is sitting by the roadside touting his black coffee
In tins painted with a tropical rainforest and a nearly naked beauty
The unbridled verdancy of the forest
And the nearly half naked blackish-red beauty just like him
Highlight certain secret tendencies unconcealable even by his excessive taciturnity

The coffee-hawking outlander comes to our city
A mere border city not far from the demarcation line
With no one drinking coffee or tea or even well water
Except the water from melted snow and ice tucked away in leather bags last winter

The coffee-hawking outlander unable to sell his coffee
Has sunk to the roadside with scarce pedestrians just like a lonely islet
Just like his lonely hometown island sunk into an uninhabited boundless ocean afar
Just like his melancholy gaze occasionally sparkling with a glow
From under his blackish-red forehead

Sinking slowly without anger or clarity
With a border city marked by his own borderline
In the quietude unique to the slow dust and time

Situations of a Bird and Two People

To the north of the North   spacious and remote
Passing through legends about rare birds exterminated by hunters
A crow is blown thither by a gale in a skew-askew manner
From the endless blank of the celestial dome

Abandoned to the bowels of the earth like a speck of seed
I have matured gradually
And acquired some kind of countenance as of a beast
Which I wish could abruptly hearten
A dejected tree from its dispiritedness
And could continuously divulge heaven's secrets
To some extent

Propelled by a gale   a child astray in the city
Remains reticent   like a long extinct species of animal
Loves to walk alone in the shadows
Or clamber up the telegraph edifice in the city hall square
Under the cover of a dead night with everything quiet
To shout and yell for a while
And then return to his sound slumber in a subway passage
Like an unkempt elf

How Did Four Dung Beetles Easily Take Away Earth

To begin with   four dung beetles from a cartoon story
Hollowed out Earth as if emptying a ball of donkey dung
And then under the cover of a dead night with everything quiet
Strained every muscle to go through all the fuss
Of attempting to furtively transport it to another place

Then there came a strange plague
Like an imaginary foe with indiscernible whereabouts
The four dung beetles were killed first   with their legs up in the air
It was a bizarre wind   not blustering but permeating
Wherever it passed by
Leas withered   forests spontaneously combusted
Rivers dried up   seas and their cerulean blue
Impetuously sank
As if being loaded into a filter funnel

Sinking together with the oceans were
Arctic and Antarctic ice crusts and snowcapped summits
They were dwindling   subsiding
Then tirelessly taken to an infinite altitude by thick fogs
To paint the firmament's azure blue into grayish blue

America   China   and Russia
Europe   Asia   and Africa
Caucasians   Asians   and Africans
All of these enemies once truer than the truth   nowadays
Are hiding under their own pergolas like imaginary foes
Without hurting each other   or knowing
Each other's whereabouts

III

A COORDINATOR'S CANYON

A Coordinator's Canyon

I was once a bird-driving man
In the bowels of the northern mountain range
From one summit to another
One canyon to another   one forest to another
Constantly coordinating the relationship
Among birds   between birds and woods
Or the cold deities and steaming hot incense in temples
Or the people with the Chinese zodiac of the goat or tiger
Lurking in a grassland
I even had to coordinate the relationship
Between the sun   the moon   the stars and others
And their relationship before and after a mist

I used not only a rod   but also a language

Those birds having grown up with my words
Sometimes flew to the South in flocks and flights
(It'd be another story if some of them perished from broken wings
While traversing the Qin Mountains)
In the South   where the birds landed
They would always awaken some mountains and rivers
However other mountains and rivers
Were continuing with a kind of sleep existent since ancient times
So the birds fond of chirping
Would also helplessly yet quietly stroll in the quietude
Without disturbing them

In the northern alps I once engaged for a long time
In the work of driving birds   conversing with them

Waiting for various species of birds
In different seasons   in all directions
To fly to and fro

Shadows

A mountain overly lofty
(Such as Mount Everest even unreachable by planes and thick fog)
You can by no means observe its shadows

A bird soaring too high
(If it loves to fly beyond the clouds like a plane)
You cannot discern its umbra

An ocean with vast blue so close to infinity
(That a whale is having fun in its deep darkness)
Similarly you can't spot its shade

However if inside your innermost heart live shadows
(And you want to eradicate them like weeding)
You must journey afar to find mountains' shadows   birds' umbrae
And the ocean's shade

Plane-Building Countrymen

The firmament has greeted birds and planes
Those who mistake or imagine birds as planes
Are not children
But urbanites

Likewise those who mistake or imagine planes as birds
Are not children
But urbanites

I recollect years ago by the Yellow River
Two brothers building a wooden airplane   my neighbors
Occupied the precipice during the day like eagles
Waiting for the dead of night with deathly stillness
To work over and over on the timber taller than a house

Only now have I understood
The brothers cut off by the great river and cliff
Are far more imaginative than we are
Growing up in the shadows by eating elm leaves
On the two banks of the great river
And furtively infatuated with everything flying
We are also plane-building countrymen

The firmament has greeted birds and planes
And someday in the future   will greet some unkempt people
Who are plane-building countrymen
But not urbanites

How to Transform into an Urbanite

Many times
You have to like a thief
Go out at night and return home in the morning
Sneak back to Hometown on a dark late night
Take out both autism and well water
Squash old clothes heirloom utensils only namable in a dialect
And a pair of pliers brought along back to your hometown
All into a canvas backpack
And then carry it alone

If in the darkness right before dawn
You still cannot haply escape
In order to handle those strangers dwelling in the village
(They all know Father)
You have to await the opportunity to transfer outward
As if pulling decayed animal carcasses
Your physical characteristics whereabouts
And countenance as of a sneaky rat
In the darkness and the rustles
Of pine needles and leaves falling to the ground from an old tree
Having withered since last year

It is possible to remove a dry well
But will the well water like a ghost
Still lurk deeper than before waiting for a slumber many years later
In which to keep pushing you down

As an urbanite your baggage is overly heavy
Before entering the city you have to
Stop at the highway service station for a long time

Carefully wash your face   look at yourself in the mirror
And then tow the heavy baggage   as if dragging the cadaver
Of a rare animal   while slinking back into the city
In the early morning

Horse

You are the one
Born in an era with no one riding horseback anymore
Fated to be a lifelong loner

Foreordained to be a wild horse   racing around
Indifferent to meadows   with no purpose
Running until you cannot run anymore

One with talents but no values   starving
Galloping   hunkering down
Indolent and free in the wilderness

One watches wildflowers
Too tired even
To take more bites of grass

You are the one
Who   when becoming an old nag
Miserably kithless and kinless   skinny and bony
Still cannot stop
Running over and over and over
Ceaselessly

A wild horse like you
Has the destiny of a horse

A horse's kismet

Tenebrosity

The tenebrosity I am talking about is pretty coquettish
Like a sodden fairy who can become so mature
Only at night as to have a charming and graceful bearing

With the sultry fragrance of tulips
It has beaten down an old lion escaping from a zoo
And its tiny exquisite yet relaxing slumber
Stranded on the roadside

The pretty coquettish darkness
Has a thin rope-like waist only deserved by a fairy
When the pretty coquetry as of a rope
Shows up in the indolent twilight
And starts to exert the effort as of a python
A beacon will be slowly suffocated

And so will be a city   in the violent aroma of tulips
In the scent wafting here from an artificial park lake
Mingled with the smell of mud

Man Studying His Own Shadow

The outlander clearly somewhat neurotic
Came from spring with a wide-brimmed safety helmet
And then performed tasks in an open space in the outer suburbs
Enjoying hiding his face in the shade of his shoulders or his visor

Facing away from the sunshine all day and every day
Was the silhouette of him hunkering down on the ground
While ceaselessly tinkering like carefully tending a swath of lawn
Frequently taking out some knives   detectors or the like
Or spending the whole day alone gesturing   muttering   even
  musing
As if embarking on an extraordinary excavation project

This unnatural man worked on the wasteland from spring to
  summer
Crouching down and standing up in a manner that exposed his
  tallness and calmness
When he grinned from ear to ear   his square white teeth would be
  revealed
And so would the flickering shadow mounting on his face from time
  to time

However this mannered fellow disappeared abruptly at the onset of
  autumn
As if having vanished into thin air
Nevertheless that large expanse of wasteland left wholly intact
  proves that
From spring to summer   he was only working in the tussocks of
  grass
Without ever hurting the ground or underground matters

Not till later did I realize: the man departing back for the city only
in the dead of night
And swerving rapidly into the shadows whenever encountering any
artificial light
Is actually a simple man   so burdened by his own shadow
And driven beyond the limits of forbearance
As to perform a rite in the wilderness to find a plan
To completely escape his own shadow

Helmsman

The cellist of the Dream Factory band is inquiring about his whereabouts
And so is a northern hermit
With his thoracic cavity depleted of deposited sand grains by a fierce gale
In a slumber I become a child holding a shuck in his hand
Inquiring of a swarm of sailors about to escape to the ocean about his whereabouts

Solitude is a fragment of a steamer
Just like a shard of a soul backlogged on the bottom of an old warehouse
And evaporating alone salt and ocean water in the depths of time and tide
Just like middle-aged me becoming an apprehensive child in slumberland
Abandoned by a man like his father or a helmsman
Chased by the surrounding twilight as rough and suffusing as seawater
And hastily rushing back to the map labeled with his hometown in the old era

Story of Searching for Spring in the Suburbs

1

The suburbs are desolate

However shortly after I arrive at the mountainside
Pervaded by the scents of the wilderness
Spring comes   peach blossoms bloom
Even a clumsy cumbrous bulldozer is approaching

Spring's peach blossoms are so splendid
And so is the shy bulldozer covered by a piece of red cloth on top

2

Deeply buried under the ground is a city
With steel pipes with bent fittings on the verge of decay
While enshrouded in the bowels of a metropolis mightier and more rigid
Is the earth   with rotten pieces like furtive territorial separatists
And sewers separately transporting more mud and turbid water
A pipe coerced by more underground tunnels
And having eaten only too much to almost burst
Is painfully stranded in the suburbs
By a stray bulldozer

3

I am in the suburbs to enjoy the peach blossoms

However the bulldozer I've encountered   dilapidated
With rusty violence and ferocity
With a driver crouching down in the cab snoozing

Just like an ailing old hen
Has prematurely opened up the old world
Hidden deeper than spring
Hence terminating in a timely manner
My journey to spring and peach blossoms

Encounter with an Enigmatic Fish

Like a bird   water
Is living inside a boulder
This fish is also like a bird
Living in the water
Crouching down like a bird's nest
In the depths of the boulder

Now this stark naked fish
Extracted by me from the rock
Gets gripped by the wind and my hands

Oh this fish looking as ominous as a strange bird
Yet rendering people in heavy contemplation
I don't think I should take it out of the mountains
Nor do I dare to return it to the roost-like water
Upon the flash of the idea
Of throwing it down from aloft
And sinking it into an unknown abyss
I can't help but sweat from guilt

I recollect this fish from a dream once
Gazing at me like a human
Hesitant between opening and closing its mouth
As mute as if it had lost its vocal cords
Reminding me of one night
When a kid astray on the road
Was imperceptibly weeping
Walking alone   fading in and out
In the darkness

Why Did a Psychic Meadow Die in Spring

Mountains are luxuriantly verdant
Numerous flowers are blooming in the wilderness
However the meadow in the central square
Carefully tended by gardeners just like a garden
Has plainly and expressly demised

Maybe the worms hidden underground
Since the warm winter have gnawed it to death
Or ravenous winter birds have eaten up its roots as a delicacy
Or sinister smog has distorted its soul
By taking advantage of its frailty and feebleness in winter

Actually a gardener wholeheartedly taking care of it last year
Has eaten too much poison
And inadvertently plunged to his death
In a dried-up well amid the mead
Before spring arrives

Flight

A butterfly is winging in the tenebrosity
Which when implied and enticed by a fully ripe apple
"Is like a dazzlingly variegated beast king
More capable of highlighting the white of the full daylight
Than feeble yet gentle light"

A butterfly can be as vigorous as a ferocious bird
Sail in bellows in the dark after waking up
And jump out like an ocean tide with an equally huge fishy odor
From a lurk as impassive as the deep sea
Rendering its flight an intent more accurate than that of death

The butterfly flying in the darkness is fierce
Having bypassed many things without deliberate refusal of
Unexpected collisions with other stray flying butterflies
Or the outcome of the undue collisions during flight

The inevitable plummeting
Or death

An Animal's Heart Is Desolate

An animal's heart is desolate
With dark blood uncleanable
Even by a bathtub of potion
And the tenebrosity unbleachable
Even by tap water almost saturated with
A ton of bleaching powder

An animal's heart is desolate
This desolation is different from that of the earth
But of the universe   of the earth
One glitter-glistering on the blade of a eunuch
Capable of killing without bloodshed
That are all startled out by a villain
With a grinning Chinese gavel
After he has transformed his genitals into a prop
And input the sperm and eggs of men and women
Beyond reproduction into a prank masquerade

An animal's heart is desolate
Without grievance   gratefulness   or happiness
When no more knives   but the entire city and its
Hush-hush underground factories and machines
And even hallucinogens and poison
Are used to kill it

Your heart and mine
Are gradually becoming desolate as well

Yatter-Natter About Poetry and Biology

Gongdu Little Heng a few other people and I
Are at the Green Island Café outside the West Straight Gate
Some are sipping tea some are drinking coffee
Others are only too bored to suggest
We talk about issues other than poetry
Yet interesting for sure

Gongdu says he is researching
The connection between poetry and biology
As it's important to examine
Whether or not poetry is still alive
And how long it can indeed live

Having just returned from a trip to North Korea
Little Heng says night there is so quiet
With a very clean city not only people
But also lights go to slumberland early

He has also mentioned many other places Libya
Syria Pakistan Cuba
And the recent situation of some people such as
Bin Laden whose body was never found
(Compared to Gaddafi how dignified it is)

Then I suddenly recall something
Instantly enlightened after touching my occipital area
And say I remember
The Bible may be missing one sentence—

Only by growing poetry and roses in the devil's belly
Can it be the warmest safest

Hometown and Pearl

1

The man I once saw pulling a piece of iron from fire
Is Blacksmith Liu Second   who can grab
A piece of red-hot iron from a charcoal fire
Throw it onto an anvil and vehemently hammer it
In his entire life   he has never stepped out of the village
But wielded an iron hammer to strike out scattering sparks
Never married a woman
But clutched a piece of iron in his hand
And furiously thrown it down   into the blaze
Oh he   livid-faced   exerted himself so vigorously
To wield up and down a hammer
As to shock rivers and mountains
And throw me out of my slumber in the bowels of the city
Again and again   even many years later

2

I once made the acquaintance of a man
Surveying the land in the wild mountains
Proficient in the secrets of plucking various wildflowers
Smiling enigmatically before vanishing mysteriously
He secretly composed a book named
The Classic of Storing Flowers
Accidentally I took a sneak peek at a few lines:
"A good flower is like a pearl   whoever
Picks its splendor should feel as if facing formidable poison
Should never tread on or damage it
With a heart-tugging mind-blowing aroma
It should be gingerly culled   cautiously taken home

Well sustained with translucent spring water
Whichever flower has a fragrance not dissipating for three days
Can be entrusted with a soul
Whichever flower has petals unwithered for seven days
Can be endowed with a body . . ."
Nevertheless I was a coarse man after all
Thereafter   whenever I saw a flower
I would feel confronted by a powerful enemy
Flee pell-mell like a frightened rat
As if chased by a strange spellbinding thing
Until one day I completely ran away from my hometown

3

I once taught myself astrology   attempting to obtain
A pearl from heaven somewhere in my hometown
But only to be told: a pearl is life-threatening
So it shouldn't be obtained

A pearl from heaven   wherever it's placed
No matter whether it shines in the wild
Inadvertently falls into the unseen dark
Or gets buried under useless land
No one should hastily touch it
"Whoever touches a pearl must perish"
This prophecy of imminent disaster
Has scared me into hurling away my astrology in a flurry
Empty-handed   and butting out forever like a potato
The village named Pearl

Notes on Visiting a Safari Park

Tiger Tiger

Tiger tiger I love you
Including what is contained in your tabby fur
Nocturnal black golden yellow
And the tangerine as sexy as a flame
Capable of burning down the entire
Empire State Building

Whilst your sabre-like teeth and fangs
With excessive tartar and an embedded iron nail
Unremovable for ages
Deserve no more white of a swan of full daylight
After the dissipation of today's smog

Peacock Peacock

Peacock peacock I love you
Including your magnificent seven-colored jigsaw puzzle
Acute toxin more lethal than snake venom hircismus
And parasites bacteria mycoplasmas
Rare and capable of overthrowing the whole city

You have allegedly had mood swings for long
With anorexia reluctant to fan out your feathers
For tourists from all over the country
Because the peahen with you
Has fallen in love with another peahen so much
So that they are determined to become homosexual
And have just run away from home

Crocodile   Crocodile

Crocodile   crocodile   I love you
Including your weeps and remorse in a northern winter dream
Having contracted a gastric ulcer
You have digested a stomachful of horseflesh
Delivered by a military horse factory
Yet unable to digest in any way
A mistakenly swallowed horseshoe

Including your sobs and fever in a northern summer dream
Due to your incessant sneaky partaking of
The tussocks of grass by a pond
And the cyanobacteria at the bottom of the pond
Those little animals just swallowed into your stomach
Are either nesting   burrowing   or dating

Including your dream in the next northern dream
Of a stark naked mermaid without a stitch on
Giving birth to a pool of knives   rods
Pieces of iron like steelyard weights
And light gray stones fitted with horseshoes

Reticent Man

A reticent man
Has inadvertently planted the best part of his vocal cords
In a field

The reticent man
Comprehends the restraint of words can make one fortunate
And how much a tree growing taller and taller
Loves rainfalls

The reticent man
Apprehends those magnificent voices are made of paper
From brutal felling
And are thereby afraid of rain

The reticent man
Has retired to home ahead of time
Pruning   watering flowers in his garden
And wandering around the hills shrouded with woods
Just like a gardener lost in his dreams

At the Back of All Things

At the back of all things   a somber tortuous place
Like Earth's mantle burned red-hot
Dominating the fate of the planet
I must search for a color
Red as lethal as the mantle   I must
Get lost for long in the red

I must become a happy achromate in the red

In the series of trifling reds of the mundane world
After endless humiliation
For seeing through neither friends nor foes
I must write a poem of gratitude with tears—

Whether lurking at the back of the red
(Maybe the back of all things)
Is weak and feeble white
Whether at the back of white
There are mists and seawater
Ebbing and flowing gently in bitterness
With the ocean and its poisoned giant whales

I know   and so do my friends and foes
It is not easy to escape the red
Unless you bake dry in fire the whole ocean
And the pines in the entire valley
And cling to it
To dance on and on

Actually the reason I am infatuated with the red

Is someday in the future
I will choose a dead-end destination at the back of things
To breathe my last happily in this red
Just for the words on my tombstone—

He has   with might and main in his lifetime
Like a sucking baby more often than not
Scraped up two trunks of Chinese red formal attire
It is worth dying for

Stranded

The starry sky's library poking out its tongue
As deformed as a dream
Has stranded excessive paper and prints
At a recycling station on a fantasy continent
With the reading of the seawater barely weighing a ton

The astronauts will never come back
The eyes of the stars close after some blinking

Now he needs sheer blankness

A Symbolist's Summer

A man covered by shiny black fish scales
A man wearing a decorative oxhorn on his head
A man with a mottled python wreathed around his waist

A man asking the moon for poison
A man having deposited an entire
Nightmare processing factory on a comet
A man having brought incantations with his quiet lone walk

Are all weird-looking men
I have never seen

Spider Is Leaving the Place You Are Leaving

A spider has left in advance
The place you are leaving

However even in a place with many people
A place with people coming and going
You still can't find
Any sign of a spider

Only at some unexpected moment
When you are alone
Will a spider suddenly appear
As for the next place it is going
You don't know

Now the place you are about to leave
A spider is departing as well
A cockroach left behind by a biological equation
(But not a gust of autumn wind)
Will mumble to itself

Now the place you are leaving soon
Has nothing to do with a spider
(Or maybe its flight)

Or the cockroaches missing for long

Discovery by a Mirror Image Researcher

A mirror image researcher is studying his own reflection
When he puts the mirror into the well water
He observes four secrets in turn—

Sometimes he is a swan   sometimes a butterfly
Sometimes a fly
Other times a mosquito

The mirror image observer is tortured by his secret mirror images
One day when he is so driven beyond the limits of forbearance
As to accidentally throw the mirror into a blaze
He spots four lines of text on the mirror burned red-hot—

A swan is the thing closest to God
A butterfly wooded mountains
A mosquito warm blood
A fly quietus

As if he had a bosomful of flames with nowhere to release
The mirror image researcher can't tell the secrets he has pried into
Thus running hither and thither in an angst and hag-ridden manner
Unable to hold back his haggardness and trance
And incapable of stopping just like a sleepwalker

He can even directly enter his dreams
Laissez-faire like an uncontrolled balloon
Wafting stumblingly around the world

Stranger Comes to Visit in a Strange Way

One night   actually in a vaguely recalled dream
He transplanted a leafy branchy yet not flowery white lilac
Into my balcony   and transformed with a vine
Hanging down from a rafter just like a rope or a green snake
My living room with a collection of
Exquisite books and carved stone monsters   into a maze
With not only glinting fireflies but also twinkling crystals

Another night   actually in another slightly remembered dream
He infinitely amplified a pot of daffodil
Nurtured by me like a treasure for many years
Turned the daffodil flower into nine   and then rendered
The nine incomparably gigantic buds
Housing sporadically nine immeasurably colossal dewdrops
Both the aroma of the flowers smellier than the odor of the sea
As if artificially nurtured   and the viscous viscid skein and tangle
More difficult to deal with
Than the humidity and elasticity contained in seaweed
Highlighted my minuteness like that of a Lilliputian from Lilliput
And caused me to hug the flower stem as huge as a celestial pillar
With dense knife-like prickles and bitterness
Just like an unfortunately abandoned Lilliputian from Lilliput
To fall into a little fit of melancholy yet helplessly desperate weeping
And then to be buried slowly by the water seeping out of a dewdrop
As vast as the vault of heaven

I know it is the tidings about a stranger's upcoming visit
Or a sign that I am leaving the city to move elsewhere
However whenever I wake up from my high-noon dream
And crane my neck to overlook outside the window

The alley where I dreamed of the lilac   maze   monstrous daffodil
Is empty without a single soul

I've never been able to see the stranger
Not even a familiar view of his strange back
Or his silhouette flashing through the distant entrance to the alley
In a haste and abrupt manner just like a mirage

IV

PLANE AND SNOW

Mary Suite No. 1

Mary   you woman
I met you last year
As well as this year
The other I beyond myself
Is captivated by you upon seeing you
Under the dim starlight of some era

Mary   I am a good boy
Only you know
I am a good boy so fond of wallowing
Only you know   oh the obsessive I
Have been worn out by chasing you
And then like a stray ghost
Let out wretched yowls
Still reverberating today
In some parts of the world

Mary   have you ever heard a man yowl-howling
Are you a good woman ever touched
By these forlorn poignant howls

Mary   a woman with tight flesh and healthy bones
Loving to look straight ahead with dazed eyes
Only knowing to walk forward
Occasionally showing a smiley yet joyless face
Never easily opening her red lips to display her white teeth
Sitting alone in melancholy among the crowd
With her sharp countenance but speechless

Mary   I have met you
As well as in my last life
A woman having dragged me into deep water like baggage
Kept me obediently still
And caused me   buried in the deepest depths
With a heart more searing than an iron block burned red
Easier to burst than a balloon
Thus more inclined to be indulged
To long to   minute by minute
Without any explanation or hesitation
Devote myself to you

Plane Descending in Raging Mist and Snow

The mist high above is enraged
And so seems the snow
Entangled and chasing with a cold current and mist
Unwilling to fall easily from the welkin
And significantly resembling the mist

I have experienced multiple times in a plane such raging mist and snow
Witnessed in person how a black eagle and a white swan
Awry into high altitude had their wings and even necks broken
Weltered thousands of times amid the icy snow and cold current
I can imagine the bloody-fleshed iced bodies from the kings of the sky
Filled up inch by inch with ice crystals
Must have been broken again and again
Then fallen in panic and disorder
Toward an anonymous territory

Raging mist and snow sometimes torture a plane
Like tormenting overshot eagles or swans
A plane unable to descend is terrified
Cut off in the firmament by raging mist and snow
Its repeated yet fruitless nosedives with some shock
Gradually stiffening your blood and heart like tearing
Are like a game about death played by God

The plane descending in raging mist and snow
Will either live or die in a split second
When God gently toggles
Between propriety and impropriety
Of the relationship between heaviness and lightness

Escaper in a Heavy Snow

With a dreadfully pale face   decent yet ghostly white clothes
In a vast white heavy snow
She sometimes ambles at a leisurely unhurried pace
Other times trots a few steps
Seemingly swallowing again and again the tears poured down her throat
And exerting more and more effort to cover up
Her strange countenance almost exposed on the street
(As a matter of fact she may be a beauty)

In the vast white heavy snow of the late dark deep of night
She abruptly appears as if escaping
Dashes straight ahead without any scruples or misgivings
Along the mortuary of the municipal hospital
(Haunted even in full daylight)
With her somewhat impetuous hot body
Which enables the heavily snowy city and ice-glazed street
To reel ceaselessly in bone-biting coldness

Like a white fox having inadvertently reincarnated
With deeply injured cauma and suspicion
And escaping swiftly yet impassively just like a mirage
From one kind of white to another

Seven-Stringed Zither Made of Old Wood[5]

As long as she wants to
She would just live in a seven-stringed zither

Made of old wood
Exuding the scent of old wood
With a soul expunged of worms
Eroded only by moonshine and wind
But compensated by her solitude and weeps

Yet when winter arrives
The aroma of the old wood will slowly sink deep
The seven-stringed zither just relishes being enveloped in dust
And playing the flicking scratches of a lighter
As well as soporific and drowsy melodies
Drab yet eccentric

5. The guqin (古琴; pinyin: gǔqín), literally meaning "ancient stringed instrument" and also called the seven-stringed zither or the ancient zither of China, is the modern name for a plucked seven-string Chinese musical instrument of the zither family.

Snow-Chasing Girl

A snow-chasing girl is shouting her loudest
Revealing the ferity surprising herself
On a whim she jumps in a heart-thrilling manner
From the summit of one edifice to the top of another
With the ethereality of a flying swallow
She even calls to the yonder mountains hazed in windy snow
Unintentionally echoing the last moan of an old mole
(Who just came home last night in the blizzard
And nearly fell to its death when traversing a precipice)
Going to hibernate and bidding adieu to the hollow mountains

The girl chased by the snow
Is wildly chasing the snow
She is galloping loose on the street shrouded with immense snow
And overrunning toward the suburbs into the tenebrosity
Of the falling dusk and the dim gloomy outskirts and wilderness
Shining with the reflections of the vast white snow
Whilst at the moment deities have gone home to rest
And the pretty coquettish female ghosts with disheveled hair just like her
Are all quiet and hiding deeply without a single soul to be seen

The girl chased by the snow yet crazily loving the snow
Suddenly becomes undaunted tonight
She cups a thick layer of snow in her hands to wash her face
And to take in mouthfuls of snow
Praying to heaven to subdue the burning flush suffusing her cheeks
And to pacify her wildly beating heart

The snow that keeps piling up in the dark is so graceful
The tenebrosity and the snow are so wan yet so cozy and lovely

That she even takes out a mirror and looks into it again and again

Rose Giver

During the day I gave the roses from her
And a large pile of old useless articles to the janitor
And smiled heartily at the back of him as he left in high spirits
Laden with all he could carry
At night I dreamed of her complaining   nagging
And tirelessly recounting her story about
Her collection of a houseful of plastic mannequins and plaster figurines

In the dream the way she rapidly vibrated her lips was similar to the way
The overcrowded fish in the tank scoured it for air
Her countenance stiffened by excessive lip gloss and skin cream
Was bitter with fright
Dissociating me from my dream as if distracting my attention
Just like a glass of water dissolving sugar crystals

Then in the next dream
I dreamed of a match   as huge as a tree stump
With a thick black made-up neck between its red head and white stalk
Seemingly expressing some kind of uncontrollable implication

Ever since then I have never again dreamed of that bunch of roses
Or the rose giver

Eternal Regret

In that era woods were luxuriant
Therefore all tigers and wolves preyed on humans

In that era men made a living by killing snakes in the mountains
So all good women washed clothes for white-faced eunuchs

In that era there was a shortage of iron
As a result there wasn't any good knife

A Snow-Loving Boy Is Nourishing Hatred in Snow

A little boy from the countryside yonder
Fond of snow   lags far behind
On his way out of school after a snowfall
The snow-loving boy   with his heart itching for action
At present by no means loves the freedom of the snowflakes
Or the fluffy thick pure white of the snow landing on everything
Instead the vigorously stirred mire covering the entire street
Capable of tripping everyone

Zheng Damao once stripping his trousers in the bathroom
Drawing a picture of his virilia and posting it on the blackboard
For others to view   should fall over
Li Kui having thrown stones at his head on the way out of school
Broken his medius and snatched the only *yuan* from his hand should slip
Yang Maochang   his math teacher calling him
A rustic   wretch and idiot in a self-study class   should trip too

He is waiting to see them make a fool of themselves
Has spotted one   two
And several strangers unknown to him   each with a muddy look
Frozen straight and seemingly tattered trouser legs
And a countenance with a color as of an eggplant

The snow-loving boy is nourishing in the snow
His hatred as shabby and clumsy as a cartoon toy

The lovely snow-loving little boy
So underclothed as to be on the verge of being frozen

Will keep waiting   keep watching
All the urbanites trip and fall into the slushy mud

Snow's Language Awakens in the Tenebrosity

Having forcefully dampened the entire winter
And secretly chilled it to the bone   the snow is slowly plummeting

Without delay   an airliner is gradually descending
Snow is subduing the friction between the steel and air
Rendering the plane's almost silent flight
As a fairy tale long forgotten
Or a scene only belonging to another world
Hoarded by a sad heart for ages
Now with its cabin door slowly opened by a blizzard

Snow is slowly wafting down from the firmament
The snow-like part of my body starts to squirm
Like a fetus inside a gravida's belly about to be delivered
Conveying the feelings of sharp pain one after another
Just like a woodpecker pecking wood

That is a language as light as snow
Falling slowly with snow after snow
That is the rigidity lurking in my body yet unleashed by the snow
Swifter and fiercer than a woodpecker's sharp beak
Nowadays its putrescent dust-sealed door leaks everywhere
Oh the snow penetrating unchecked
My body and the darkness in my heart
Has opened the door to the language
And its entire world's
Wide openness and falsity

Legendary Bad Girl

When you put on a red dress
(Which actually didn't have to be too red)
You became a legendary red fox
So pretty and coquettish as if you couldn't be any more bewitching
When you were attired in a white dress
(So decently white)
You were a white swan
With elegant grace and tallness complementing each other
And some nearly unreasonable hauteur
Only choosing to loiter occasionally in an unknown heavenly lake
And flying at a height unreachable to others for half a lifetime
As of the blue higher than a plane
When you pulled on black clothes
You became a lively vivid black fairy
Loving to play pranks besides being missish
You witnessed those occasionally tempted by you
Fall into the water like drowning dogs
But felt sympathy for them
Signaling proficient swimmers to their rescue
When everything settled in harmony and peace
You were still yourself making no disguise of your sly grin
Which only belongs to a dark fairy packing up your bags
And leaving alone in a slow stately manner

You were once a legendary bad girl but nowadays
Those rumors and tidings false and phony
Talked about and circulated under the table
You live in another house to deliberately stay away from them
As if having invited a deity you dress up nicely only for a mirror
In this life some of those things in your fate

Some running creeks   some verdure and verdant lushness
Only concealable by lofty mountains
The red and white only legends deserve
And the profound black set off by the white unsurpassed in the world

You have said   these are the only things and truthfulness
Left in your simple life
When alive   you only stay with them
And so will you upon your demise

History of Hypnosis

To them   poetry has become
A kind of outdated legend—

Legend says poetry is merely an insect's uglyish carcass
Or the cadaver of an ant
With a dead look similar to that of a child
Due to its metamorphic development
That has been dragged deep into a desert by another insect
And then stranded there

Legend says in order to find it   a bird
Has broken its wings and sunk in the sand in a sultry blast
A lizard is on its way to find it
And has strayed from its path while walking

To them   poetry has transformed into the beginning
Of a history of slumber more and more obese—

Outside the door to a choir   he lets out a fat greasy belch
Even plus another one smelling of rotten food overnight
At the moment of thinking
All these things happen successively in midsummer
In the desert with rolling sizzling heat waves and impassable ways
Slowly   drowsiness strikes him
He starts to snore

A poet and his neighbors have fallen asleep
And so has time

Photo of Free Life in the E-Era

Young as he is   he has a weird personality as of a widower
Living in a shabby shade shack in an urban village
Alone with a computer
Running a few supermarkets on the Internet
And accompanied by a plastic mannequin

He has never taken any woman home
Legend says he occasionally mates with the mannequin

And that in the torrid heat of last summer or the summer before
They gave birth to a genetic freak
A patient of obesity with the buttocks of an elephant
A horse's neck   an ox's horns   a bird's beak
And some other uncertain features

If he hadn't been driven so mad by the torridity
As to rush out of the shack
Into a frozen food processing plant in his dream
And knock over the thin door
Exposing all the dirty secrets of the legend
He and the mannequin would still be the sweetest couple
In the diminishing torn-down urban village
Their life hidden with many legendary little secrets
Would still bewilder those peepers unable to have their way

The Snow Belonging to You Will Slowly Fall

The snow belonging to this universe will slowly fall

The world having fully suffered humiliation
Is waiting at Four-Way Intersection
And so is the worn door sign of an old *yamen*[6]
Tormented by an arrogant "turned-up belly"
Plus those notorious things in all forms accumulated
Since last year or the year before last
With frequent clicks and squeaks
As of fish blowing bubbles or an old cat threatening a mouse
With anxious preoccupation and an itch for a try
More resounding than the sound of mating
They are waiting
To be excited in the snow by the inexplicable dampness
Which grows more lethal with each passing moment

The snow belonging to the language of this world will gradually fall

The speed of the slow-falling snow is the speed of the language
The snow of the language or the language of the snow is gradually
Expunging the dark despicable and filthy parts of matters
And also the part of the language as furry-fuzzy as the snow
Shedding all those fluffy unbridled embellishments
And transforming the entire world into a verb
Not only somewhat impetuous but also slightly overbearing
A powerful verb or a noun with the texture of a verb
Narrating the snow more accurate than a noun and more sensitive than a verb

6. A *yamen* (衙门; pinyin: yá mén) was the administrative office or residence of a local bureaucrat or mandarin in feudal China.

You a little woman a snow belonging to you will slowly fall too
The snow as lighthearted and foul-smelling as your wildcat temperament
Smelling the same as your perfume as secretly tantalizing as your body scent
Unable to nip its gaffe in the bud due to its excessive coquetry
With its flying white unable to suppress the flush dancing on your cheeks
Rushing toward another little woman
With the lightness as of a feather and incomparable charm
Losing its fundamental equilibrium because implicit vitality
Continuously overcomes the weight as of lead
Peeling off the oppression of the whole winter
As if eliminating shyness on the first wedding night

You a little woman or a little man smaller than a little woman
The snow belonging to you will slowly fall
Just like the snow belonging to this world and its language
Gradually plummeting ingeniously yet somewhat brutishly

Normal University Graduate Shangguan Yunyun and Her Anecdotes

Shangguan Yunyun   a graduate of a normal university
Was assigned to teach at a primary school in the desert
Where she couldn't find a whole lawn
With her skinny scrawny appearance
Exactly like that of a time-worn pointer
Contemplative yet slightly hesitant
Just like a leaky outdated machine tool

Oh in the dimness of a classroom echoing a survived impasse
Or an old factory building   that couldn't be any older
She opened a heavenly book   thinking that
She couldn't open the many students   smaller machines
Thus shouted again and again
Regardless of time and space soundly sleeping

"She is driving the taxi of biology toward a strange place"

Perched on a log bench were five or six bird-like children
Teaching four or five courses alone   proficient in all
Shangguan Yunyun was an all-rounder in the hearts of all
Just like the shadow behind the town
With no one caring or judging
Whether it was long or short   rose or fell

Whilst her features were so explicit   to begin with her hair
Was short and strong   very much like a man's
Interspersed with her postures were those revealing sleep deprivation
An enigmatic quality

Oh legend says her emaciation known far and near
Was a kind of terrible disease

"I will drive the taxi of biology toward a strange place"

I recall she was once my physiology teacher at primary school
Loving to pucker up her plump lips while lecturing
With very red ear rims and super white teeth
While squatting to eat a meal cooked on a large stove for everyone
She would protrude her big buttocks quite disproportionate to her thinness

I recollect many prestigious men were kept out by her
With her poor vision   she often spilled a bottle of red ink at night
I dare say the red-stained toilet paper was irrelevant to menses
Nevertheless I dare not say
Her celibacy was the result of her early cohabitation with a man
As a spinster   she abhorred the mating and procreating of this era

"To drive the taxi of biology to a strange place"

Lonesome Tiger-Rearing Girl

A lonesome girl can't nurture flowers
Because of her excessive endogenous heat
No matter how much water and dew
Are poured or sprayed on a pot of flowers
They will suffocate with wilted stems and leaves
In as short as one week

A lonely girl can't nurture flowers
So she turns to raise a tiger
In the way of rearing a pet
But only to find out
The best way to raise a tiger is to starve it

She starves it in a cage for long persecutes it
Stares directly at it in silence from a distance
Until the intolerably ravenous tiger eventually
Not only eats meat but also gulps mouthfuls of
Vegetables and grass without being picky

The tiger reared by the solitary girl
Devouring not only meat but also grass and vegetables
Extremely famished
Has more vigor and gusto and even more frenzy
Than the average tiger

Girl Coerced into a Snowy Night and Its Vacancy by a Dream

Snow is coming
The girl chasing the snow simultaneously with her dream and body
Feels the icy coldness of an apple on her
And thereby weeps furtively

She alone is building a snowman in the backyard of an institution
Wearing a red overcoat and green pants
She just wants to dress more glamorously
Yet the colors associated with dreams
A small portion of her not being beautiful enough
Are nearly betrayed or inappropriately exposed
By her body becoming hotter and hotter during work
Due to her overly thin clothes
To be dedicated to the snow

The girl loving to be neat and clean   with mysophobia
Is torturing feather-like snowflakes
After work the snowy ground is a backdrop
For her reckless and dangerous gallop and nearly uncontrolled haste
She just wants to shout her loudest
Rush into her house together with the snow with the same
   recklessness
And in the fully energetic pent-up scent
Of old clothes and a camphorwood cabinet

Arrange piece by piece the colors of dreams
From under the old days with tons of old overstocked stuff

Fish-Shaped Snow

Through the stained glass window of an old post office
I retrieved the snow burned hot by your scarlet fever
From a safe in a secret base of the Space Agency
I brought back the snow you deposited last year
From the umbrage of a lawn persistently unwilling to die
I fetched an evergreen spindle like a betrayer's face
And the gloomy snow hidden deep for it
From the cover of an old magazine from an aged newsstand
Depicting a black-and-white snowscape
I got back the snow as despicably filthy and nasty as darkness

However tonight's snow   mingled with the shards
Of furtively disintegrated starshine
Will drop all the forms almost decayed to nothing
And in the blush of a terribly ashamed gravida
Pile up without any disguise   the dreamed dust
And all its fish-shaped moisture

Nocturnal Singer

A nocturnal singer is in the yonder
As far-flung as the depths of your heart
Successfully reachable only if death arrives

The nocturnal singer doesn't ride on a train
Instead he walks forward in the direction of the tracks
Nor does he take a bus
Instead he heads forward along the road
Nor does he fly by plane
Instead he loves to chase the whereabouts of soaring birds
As to how he simultaneously migrates with the birds
From one place to another
It has never been known to anyone else
Just like a secret of a somnambulist

The nocturnal singer   far away
Is singing in praise of another person
One with a tranquil attitude as if praying
And one forever in a nonlocal place
Courageous   insightful and as serene as usual
Even in the quietude

I sympathize with the nocturnal singer
And the person sung about by the singer
With all his slightly unsociable and eccentric
Composure and solitude

Mary Racked by the Moon and Snow

Mary   a good girl   lives
In a mirror wrapped in a yellow silk shawl
After returning from work
Tidying up her hair bun and sticking a flower in it
She exposes in the mirror her smiles indicating her refusal
To have a motive
She is rejoicing that she passed through the main street
All the way with the speed of a somnambulist
And that   under the starlight models at the gate
Of the old post office by the Bell Tower
She turned on her earphones and radio so rapidly
As to exclude all the hurly-burly and hubbub of the past
And the secret dust seemingly wafting down from the moon

Mary   a good girl   has as much purity and suspicion
As a swallow   but never reveals them
She fell in love with me the year before last
And enjoyed soliloquizing under the starry sky
She was in love with me last year
And stole the moon and mists from the unfathomable blue
But inadvertently lost her footing
And fell into the entire vacancy of her pinewood drawer

This year Mary   as indifferent as a nation hidden in an old castle
Is alienating me as if she had been out of town
From spring   to summer   and to autumn
I pretend to mow grass to see her
Mary   a word more difficult to pronounce
Than with tears stuck in my throat

From her garden   again and again
I was rejected   aggrieved and crestfallen

Mary   a woman tortured by the moon and snow
I read your serenity and missishness in the mirror
Winter has come   and so will the snow according to legend
I will choose to see you in snowy weather
Come together with snow
And hold my guts and tears more honest than a rock

While watching you from a recess unseen by you

Mirror

You tell that man
He will forever stay out
Even though he is so infatuated with a snow
That he hides in snow
And even has buried his own demise
In a not-so-unexpected avalanche
For hiding too deep

A blizzard is destined to happen outside
The man can't contain his delirium in the blizzard
The silently and swiftly accumulating white
Is chasing his reticent gallop

When he gradually depletes his body of water and flames
In the thickness   depth and quietude of the snow
And when the scale on the mercury tube of his body
Allows the in-depth step-by-step inquiries from the icy snow
And its hibernation with dreams together

You tell that man
Ready to dedicate or even sacrifice his life
He still remains outside
And so do the snow and smiles entrusted by death
With bewildered countenances seemingly astray

Quietude and Mysophobia

His study is too clean and tidy
Even for a mosquito to land
Somewhat fancy   somewhat unreal
I don't like it

Her countenance is too clean-cut and natural
Even for a speck of dust to fall on without feeling abashed
Obviously she is relatively sensitive and missish
I really like her

V

MOUNTAIN ALWAYS WORSHIPPED BY ME

Mountain Always Worshipped by Me

The mountain always worshipped by me
Aging in the sunshine and moonlight
Growing taller day by day with people on its back
Standing straighter than a sword
Washed immaculately clean
By thick fogs and long continuously blustering gales
Having to be ascended section by section in several eras
Rendering one's heart growling ceaselessly on his brow
You must scale it in person
And pass your hand over it
At a high place where you are stranded
Just like a silent father touching his son's vertex
With rumpled-tumbled hair before parting
Or a son having returned
Reuniting with his father after so long
And touching the old weak frontoparietal region
Of his aged father in the same way

The mountain I have adored all the time
Exclusively composed of rocks
Which I often want to climb up for a walk
However busy I am and however little time I have
I will surely find time
(Sometimes in spring   but more often in autumn)
To shinny it up to a high place or higher
(For five minutes at least   or an hour at most)
To look at it   again and again
And to touch it   again and again

Until my body temperature seems to gradually dissipate
In the cool breeze at high altitude
And my tears irrepressible even with reticence
Trickle down my cheeks

Ballad of Clouds and Mists

A majestic valley is always mantled
By clouds and mists just like the Qin Mountains
Those untraversed regions
Are nurturing the rare and peerless beauty as of autism
And as of an impasse
You can't help sinking into once you enter

I know nowadays the ways of the world have changed
Most or part of life will remain shrouded in smoke
The city is always smoky and murky
Because a lot of people from afar
Flood elsewhere with shouts and clamors
Before their bottoms warm up the seats here

I also know not only the Qin Mountains
But also more mountains or something else colossal
Beyond the Qin Mountains
Are enshrouded with clouds and mists
And even stand erect beyond clouds and mists

The Qin Mountains: The Seven States of the Boulder Manor

1

You can't move these boulders home
They are irrelevant to whether
You are a landowner   a wealthy farmer or a capitalist
And so are they to your yard

They are beyond you and me
Outside wind and time
But within God's courtyard

Compared to these boulders
A bird flying over the Qin Mountains
A blade of grass and a tree growing here
Are all accidental
And fortunate

2

To find the boulders always calling for people to understand
Generations upon generations of people overshoot so much
Stay away from home for so long   venture so deep
As to stray in the mountains and among the boulders
Real   reticent   haughty   as strange
As newborns every time they meet them

3

No matter how a boulder is opened
More right angles   edges and corners are opened up

One or numerous right angles   edges or corners
As shiny as a knife
Foreshadow more dangers surprisingly unexpected
Or nonexistent at all

4

These boulders also have a deep-hidden sense of humility
Occasionally you can have a close run-in
With their curvature and serenely charming territory
In such boulders
The right angles   edges and corners
Simply have abandoned their hidden sinister motives
You can explore deep into them to find out more coquetry
Accumulated in the depths of the boulders is water
As smooth and fine-textured as a mirror
This never-used mirror seems to be waiting for you as always

Now you can try looking at your face in it
To see whether
It's the face of a horse   a ghost   or a human

5

You can break the boulders
Just like a chivalrous man
With a heartful of abashment and remorse
Fracturing his own bones
In the martial arts world of ancient China
And then singing against the wind

Rendering the snapped boulders
Revealing more straightness as of a fang

When daggers are drawn and sabers rattling
There must be something rolling into a ball
Just like a tiger having swallowed an acute toxin
Landing in spasms and twists

However those broken boulders are an exception

6

The straightness of the boulders is plainly obvious
And untransformable

Not only unyielding
But also arrogant

Whether their directions
Are upward or downward
Or slanted with an angle
The boulders are straight

The unwieldiness   perfect rotundity
Or peaceful seclusion
Of their concealed unpredictable straightness
Is going to unhurriedly tell you a story
Of a mountain   as straight and direct as a sword
Of time   of white clouds   of birds
Or hidden in roots

7

Towering boulders have transformed into mountains
Wild   never tame for anyone
Having enchanted the wind and a bird

Unable to be taken away by you
And rendering you and your taciturnity
Most willing to become a beast
After going astray

Eulogy to the Qin Mountains

The mountains with trees and grass growing casually
Simple and unadorned   with massive boulders
Blustered down by gales and then perching
With the momentum of ferocious birds
On riverbanks   on precipices   in exuberant grass
In the depths of the dim silent light of night
Or in an untraversed place

Oh the mountains looming in and out of the thick mists

Casually changing every day   rustic and pristine
Guarded like secrets by broken cliffs   fallen boulders
And soaring birds   with expeditions and recluses
Hustling and bustling with unknown whereabouts
Capable of arousing inexplicable melancholy in a sightseer
Strolling in the far suburbs with a casual glimpse

Render time   history and eras
As a lenticular cloud wafting over the mountains
As to which is lighter or heavier   it's beyond weighing

Elaborating on the Boulders on Mount Hua

These colossal boulders rising straight from the ground
Growing taller and taller toward the sky and clouds
Having been surveyed by my ancestors and grandfather
And to be measured again by me and my son
Seem to protrude from another world
With scars and prophecies in their subtle places
Felt by the sun   the moon and the stars

Their depths are said to be uninhabitable for the heart
Except for elves
No one knows how far their roots extend in the strata
Deep in the Qin Mountains
Or whom they are talking to beyond the clouds

But an eagle knows
And so does a massive yet unnamable bird
When this and that
Once again fly over the heights as of the boulders
They know flight is a game of beauty
Which gradually approaches the extreme
Due to danger and futility

Story of Searching for Boulders on the North Mountains[7]

These boulders live together with the firmament
Birds' flying height   droppings
Reticent flights   and thick mists
If you are lucky   you will also spot them
Living with the reflections of skylight and clouds
In a heavenly lake

All of these boulders are broken
With sharpness piercing directly into the heavens

Because they contain more edges   corners and straights
Opening them
Is like opening the heart of a hermit
Or breaking a chivalrous man's back
Which is extremely dangerous

7. The North Mountains (北山; pinyin: běi shān) can also be translated as the Beishan Mountains. Together with the Qin Mountains, they divide Shaanxi Province into northern, central, and southern parts.

A Nonexistent Mountain

1

When clambering the Qin Mountains
You can't loosen your grip   or breathe a sigh of relief
Instead you must climb to the highest and most dangerous place at a stretch
The sunrise on the East China Sea overlookable from Mount Hua
The deep snow baptized since time immemorial on the acme of Mount Taibai[8]
And the azure blue gloomy for a millennium in the lakes
Those most beautiful places   when you feel like almost going astray
Will meet you unexpectedly at an extremely dangerous place

2

I have been searching for the Qin Mountains for ages
Crisscrossing the seventy-two valley entrances or more
Like a somnambulist   but can only meet their nicknames
The real Qin Mountains   are forever in a place you can't see
Or reach

3

Among the Qin Mountains   I have always been looking for a mountain
With the most suitable height   plants   animals and climate
Hermits' corpses or their body scent lingering after they have just left
That allows me to see the greatest things on both sides of the great Qin Mountains

---

8. Mount Taibai (太白山; pinyin: tài bái shān) is the highest peak of the Qin Mountains.

The Yellow River to the north   the Yangtze River to the south
Meaning ten thousand Chinese miles of yellow sand   cliffs   turbid waves
And ten thousand Chinese miles of verdancy   lucid water
Floating clouds   haze and melancholy   respectively

And to witness   how birds on both sides of the mountain
Warble mournfully and linger in the four seasons
How they   in an attempt to fly over the Qin Mountains
Go astray and plummet after extreme exhaustion
And sometimes survive haply   returning from the sides of one great river
To those of the other

4

But I know even if I search until my last breath   the Qin Mountains
Won't give me such a height   just as they have separated
The Yangtze and Yellow Rivers   two ambitious children
Rushing independently toward the ocean
Just as they watch two rivers fight with each other
Or two ferocious dragons grapple
Until they finally can't bear it
But only wipe away tears alone in the capacity of their mother

5

Now   I am getting old
But still going for broke to look for that mountain
Named the Qin Mountains   inundated by its many nicknames
Possibly nonexistent   on whose south and north
My grandfather was old   and so were my father and mother
They lived by the river and passed away one after another

My lover is old as well   and so is my hometown
Whilst the wild grass and the lake becoming a shoal in the valley
Render the white and dark clouds
Pressing down further

6

The Qin Mountains   are like a nonexistent mountain
Or a mirror   after many things vanish
And I disappear as well

Our most ideal denouement
Is to become a secret in its mirror image

Legend of Xi'an

Legend says Xi'an has been subsiding
Thus making the surrounding mountains higher and higher
The smog over it thicker and thicker
And the sun above it cudgel its brains to penetrate the smog
For at most a dozen days each month

I can never believe or accept this legend
Nor can I be satisfied with
Merely looking at the Qin Mountains in the yonder
Therefore pretending to increase outdoor workouts
I have cultivated the habit
Of climbing the Qin Mountains in their depths

Thus I know those things only contained by
The Qin Mountains: hermits   vagabond chivalrous men
Monks   outlaws   martyrs to love   misanthropes
Treasure hunters   self-cultivating men for immortality or nirvana
The living and the dead both unaware of the truth
They are   at a place higher than the mountains
Actually higher than birds and clouds
Looking down with their clairvoyance
At how I mount the mountains   how the jagged-ragged summits
Baffle me with clouds and mists
And then wake me up with a clump of gas mingled with frozen
  snow

Xi'an has become bloated and sprawling day by day over the years
And will definitely sink faster
According to the principle of gravitational acceleration
Ensuring that   in this way   the Qin Mountains

And the deities on them   all outside the wafting clouds
Rise higher and farther

Until one day they reach a place no longer reachable by a mountaineer
A place higher and farther   where the legendary Qin Mountains are
And where the subsiding legendary Xi'an
Finally stops sagging

Legendary Red of the Qin Mountains

It is the red of maple leaves and a plant
Unnamed by botanists in time
The red facing the North   of lofty mountains
And of giant soaring birds

A kind of red awakened by a gale
From the boulders
From the epilogue of autumn
From the mists
From an unaware soundly sleeping dream

The red that is nonexistent in this world
Or unclaimed
That renders the verdant moss on the white boulders
And the solar halo rising to the pinnacle of a mountain
Of ten thousand *ren* without even batting an eye[9]

That makes any convention of coquetry
And any culling and picking meaningless
That will hide the Qin Mountains and their boulders
In the celestial dome
Until after autumn   after winter
And after the colossal ice and heavy snow

In a place you will reach not by strength
To remain alone with the dizziness or vastness

---

9. *Ren* (仞; pinyin: rèn) is an ancient measure of length equal to seven or eight Chinese feet or *chi*. A mountain of ten thousand *ren* figuratively means an extremely high mountain.

The Place I Want to Go

The place I want to go
Should be surrounded by irregularly sized higgledy-piggledy mountains
On which a big bird can land without feeling indecent and a small one afraid
On top of which dark clouds tirelessly linger
When the clouds are happy   the firmament can be so blue as to be detrimental
When they are weeping   a nice rain will cast down from the heavens
Occasionally they can make a fuss by unleashing an unremitting downpour
Causing several mountains to collapse
And many birds to become badly waterlogged

Whilst the ground where I live is as thick as you could imagine
Abundant with variegated honey   legends   and a small number of monsters
Legend says the honey is like poison in that
It has drowned dynasty after dynasty in fame   fortune   frivolity   fascination
And that monsters have eaten successively several ancient little emperors
The rumors more abundant than the honey are prettily flowery and tirelessly noisy
Like wild bees   butterflies   ghosts   fairies
Nevertheless these ancient legendary things sound upsetting and annoying
Now I just want to stay here quietly and comfortably   with the four seasons
As well-defined and distinct as snow   rain   flowers   seeds
Among which the ripening season is most preferred
With impassive clusters of

Wheat   pomegranates   and a small number of paddies
All evaginated like the labia of a gravida about to give birth
Too many crops   dark clouds   birds   lazybones
And blooming poppy flowers   a bin of wet spoiled grain
A few ruined pots of rice and flour
And occasionally two or three young men going rogue

The place I want to go   is the place an emperor especially aspires to go
Refusing to leave once he gets there
Trains long to go   planes desire to go
Astronauts particularly crave to go for a walk before traveling to outer space
And even time planning to give up embracing its nihilistic mask
To become an austere serene person
Fancies hastening to directly

Seven Days in the Qin Mountains

On the first day   you saw the weeds and vines almost impassable
With somewhat excessive density and luxuriance
Which   like a half-recognized head-on blow at the first encounter
Emphasized some same familiar
Yet nameless wander and hesitation

On the second day   you witnessed a colossal boulder
Of the same ilk with the mountain ridge   with a crevice
Implicitly coincident with a certain character trait of time
(This scenario would appear again and again)
It led you to keep heading on a journey toward ruin
Or another mountain coexisting with the massive boulder
That would gradually weaken your imagination
As much as your physical strength

On the third   fourth   fifth   and sixth days
You strayed through one or numerous valleys
Besieged by gigantic boulders and forests
Without daylight or birdsong except on the return route
Dripping water wearing away a stone muttered regretfully
In unknown depths   like your heartbeat gradually slowing down

On the seventh day   on the periphery of the Qin Mountains
Mountain searchers broke the stems of an expanse of grass
And the bones of several vines and then left in succession
The news of your disappearance was like a deluge
Surging higher and higher in all versions
On TV   in newspapers   on the Internet
And among kith and kin

Afterward   like the sea once billowing with undercurrents
Or a small-scale landslide in a night-covered valley
Or something of nonoccurrence
Everything will eventually end in silence

This Summer's Qin Mountains

This summer   more people retreat to the mountains
Including more strangers   people with plans
Those who need the hidden depths of the mountains
To conceal their misdeeds and vices
And those who desire to put the corpulence of summer
Into the coolness of an alpine lake and the water of a deep ravine

There are even some people with more obvious sinister motives
Who   as more and more people enter the mountains
Become particularly restless and move each passing day
Toward the deeper part of the Qin Mountains
Like a fish having narrowly escaped the seine and fleeing to deep water

Oh Qin Mountains   this summer you have attracted so many betrayers
With bromhidrosis   hubbub   eccentric thoughts
As undetectable as the pain in the private parts
And the waste abounding in the entire valley waiting for a long-overdue
  cleanup
I don't like them   or choose to stay among them
Whether uphill or downhill

I will retreat early from the mountains   into the extremity of the earth
Beyond the horizon shrouded in brume
Or even farther than the haze and horizon

Melancholy

A train threaded its way through the Qin Mountains
Through a lengthy tunnel more imaginative than the afterlife
And then zoomed off into the yonder like an impetuous ghost
A plane flew over the celestial arc
Under this aircraft and beneath the smog
A bird repeatedly circled but unable to land
Finally winged away

I stood on the ground in amazement
Gawking at them leaving one by one   and in the end
Leaving behind only a nearly nihilistic shade of blue
Over the Qin Mountains   so nihilistic
So prolonged and blue

Plane Flying in the Desperate Blue

Above the plane is blue   and so is under it
In the infinite blue
In which even directions don't seem to exist
The plane seems to glide very slowly
This soundless and stirless yet limitless blue
Has almost controlled the shivers of the plane
Quivering it only slightly
Rendering the dazzlingly white sunshine
With some still coldness

The plane is winging in this almost desperate blue
As if it were flying over
Near-extinct nihility

Commemorating a River in Advance

This enormous river   after dwindling and degenerating
Amid sandy land   nowadays is as tenuous as gossamer
Just like a decrepit old earthworm
That keeps dragging on with a body inclined to degradation
Expanses of soughing pines as vast as a big desert
Mantling both sides of the river now have been taken elsewhere
By the wind in memory

From north to south   from west to east
The sand dunes have been slowly inching ahead
Soft yet lovely
Accompanied by some plants
Continuously alternating between withering away and regenerating
Depredating while moving as soundlessly as the body of a fire

Now all left here are the stark naked sandy land
Lizards scared from beginning to end
Mournful stumps
Shrubs never able to stand up
Sprawling on the ground like wormwood
With sinews and bones broken by gales

The North is vast   and so is the reticence
Of the northern sandy land under the scorching sun
The once enormous river   has left the earth
Its equally massive empty shell

Lurkers' Portrait

The Qin Mountains are hidden in the bowels of the sky
Whilst the latter is concealed deeper within the former
A libertarian is infatuated or content with the Qin Mountains
Stroked by the dark belly of the white clouds
He once overlooked when time was hanging heavy on his hands

Of the Qin Mountains   their perennial perpetual mists
Are only a part   and so are the rumbling river
Billowing out of a valley entrance
The limestone   lakes   massive boulders
None of which can ever wake up
And the fish unable to grow up in cold water

As well as the nightmarish lurkers
Behind the screen of gargantuan boulders
The overcast sky
And countless mountains

I Have Captured Another Monster

In these mountains   all tigers have perished
Even the stealthily prowling wolves have vanished for years
The legendary old black bear eating devils instead of men
With its gall removed by an indomitable hunter
Shuddering with a whole lot of uncontrollable fat
Has fallen to its death
Rolling down the mountain like a giant ball

Afterward a man clambers up the mountain range
To capture monsters   runs up and down for ages
And lives in the dark strata and chasms of giant boulders
Like a savage and also a deity of the mountains
Whilst the legendary monsters are all mysteriously latent
For many years   this monster hunter
Exhausts his wits in vain

One day this monster catcher   indefatigable and unflinching
Came to the city like a monster at high noon
Emanating the foul smell of a monster   during our only encounter
Looking at his monstrous appearance   I felt somewhat embarrassed
"I have captured another monster!"
The words I had been thinking about for so long
Could not be uttered in the end

Great Heavenly Deity

A great heavenly deity has planted here
Boulders   red stemmed and leafed flowers
Berries on the heads of deep grass   chills in the depths
The slumberous reticence of a black eagle and towering rocks
Accumulated snow unsteadily glitter-glistering
On the apex of Mount Taibai in June
Like the moisture-corroded face of a secluded hermit
Grasshoppers and crickets in karma and reincarnation
A shiny black river running down from the mountains
Wild boars and asthenopic bears

The great heavenly deity has planted here
Constantly lingering thick fogs
Morning glow   the great sun   the great moon
All rising to the treetops with birds
Damp   miry   putrescent yet pale faces
Abashed faces   the glistening golden face
Of a spiritually enlightened gainer and master of alchemy
And the face of the sun
Nestling amid the dark clouds
And slowly wriggling and squirming
Like the belly of a gravida

Child Loving to Go up the Hill

Many people know   in my hometown
I was a well-known restlessly untamed child
Dismayed   unsociable and eccentric
Loving to come and go singly like a lonely maverick
And enjoying going up the hill
Nevertheless many people don't know
The birds twittering alone with the moon on the alps
Every night   flew away at daytime seeming astray
During my countless trips to the mountains
Never before had I seen any real birds

They even don't know
When a gale was blowing the empty nests
And the bird droppings and withered twigs
Shaken down toward the ground
Were constantly splattering me
Countless times   as a child summoned by the birds
I could only gaze out to the yonder vastness
With pent-up melancholy in my heart

Envoy of the Semimythic Age

From one foreign land to another
I prefer to be a poet camping in the open air
Like a woman beautiful even during procreation with tacit love
I constantly surmount my hesitation and doubt
To write down those things worthy of making poetry shine
This planet vagabonding in nihility every day
And snobs' rights and wrongs   as well as splitting hairs
That are turned inside out by me with a reflective mirror

My world is another universe: in my poetry
I don't usually mention a specific country but rather a particular place
For instance   I don't write "Great Britain" but "foggy London"
Or "America" but "on both sides of the beautiful Mississippi River"
It makes me look extremely like a man
Living in the age of mythology or semimythology
Enjoying the open air
Especially the quietude under the night sky

I mean spring is right here
With beauties   fresh blossoms
Smiles as forbearing as those of paupers
And the sensual verdancy of the earth and trees
That are all simple and honest yet willful
Looking innocent wherever I go
Reflecting   like my reflective mirror   the strange land
Which I have traveled and experienced all the way
Its parochialism with swirling dust and growling machines
Its austerity and integrity not coverable even by its city walls

Oh heaven let me continue to wander at the edge of the sea
And to polish myself with a stone dipped in the seawater
Until the borders tattooed on my back in my early years are abraded
Until I finally can chant to the heavens
Flames' tangerine and the ocean's azure blue have no boundaries
Nor do exuberant vegetation and fount-like birds' warbles
Just as the nearly nihilistic blue
That cannot be forcibly occupied by
This spring seawater
The messenger of a blue star in this universe
Or even villains

Contains in its heart one or even numerous constellations
Just like a heart

VI

ROCK ARRANGEMENT

Middle-Aged Man's Self-Portrait

Sojourning by the ocean   wasting the springtime of my youth
And drinking the seawater for a whole decade (as long as a generation)
I was bitten a few times by a monster fish unknown to anyone
And entangled in blue-green algae several times after jumping into the sea
(And once nearly dragged down the abyss)
The letters I requested sailors and albatrosses to send to the ocean
Had all vanished forever like stones dropped into the sea
Drinking seawater and lapped up by waves   I waited
So long that the hair in my occipital area all slowly fell off
And the beauty as of a Lagenaria siceraria was revealed
Before all my hair became gray
Also a blue glazed porcelain cup brought from the North
Fell and broke while I was escaping a tsunami striking in a dream
Sending my dream in which I drank a stomachful of seawater
And a cluster of porcelain shards as azure blue as the ocean
To Davy Jones's locker at the same time
And failing to transform my yellow belly rubbed to and fro by the seawater
Into a seagreen-tinted blue one as I entered middle age

After wasting all the springtime of my youth by the ocean
I returned as a middle-aged man to the North   a high-altitude area
Where one can most easily give up not only resentment but also sadness
Now I live where I can look up to see the Qin Mountains afar
Next to a well where many people come to draw water even before dawn
In a zone through which an incognito river (called *jiang* in the South) flows[10]
Not far from a heavily guarded aircraft factory
A little far from a reputedly secret aircraft test base
Knowing some plane-building friends

---

10. *Jiang* (江; pinyin: jiāng) is also translated as river just like *he* (河; pinyin: hé).

And people proficient in the secrets of space flight
Now is the only little secret in my stomach besides the seawater
Nowadays my daily job is to safeguard my little secret somewhat distractedly
Like a sloppily unkempt farmer in a distant countryside
Neglecting to plow and sow   except waiting foolishly every day
With time hanging heavy on his hands and very little sleep every night

Having returned from the seashore   by tramping over hills and dales
Rolling and crawling   with youth depleted by the sea and its nihilistic azure
I came back to the north of the Qin Mountains feeling aggrieved and crestfallen
A northern area nowadays no longer engaging in careful and intensive cultivation
With no place to puke up a stomachful of bright blue seawater
With no one knowing either the reticence deeply hidden
In the almost reckless leisure day and night
Or the nearly ridiculous little secret

A Boulder on the Mountain

Across a river flowing with mud and sand
A large expanse of thorns and unknown wilderness
And the slopes of some peaks making a show of themselves
Lies the boulder on the mountain
I am fond of beholding on Sundays

Plain   with adamantine and rough edges and corners
Accompanied by some weeds
That renders people thinking about the depth it sinks into the soil
And surveying in detail its well-rounded and smooth facet
Polished by gales and sunshine
And its surprisingly unexpected crevices
Caused by an excessive lack of ingenious craftsmanship

Its mysterious swirl pattern resembles
The pugmarks shaped like plum blossoms and stamped by a giant beast
And then embellished by time
The blood of a loyalist in a dynasty
Ticktacking from a scaffold
However with its surname blurred by time diffusing away
And the smiley self-manifestation of the relieved minds
Of the dynasties having fallen to their death one by one
And taken many years to completely dissipate their white bones
And to choose this boulder on the mountain

I just like to hike on the mountain
The boulder I am going to meet
Has been placed there from ancient times to the present
Swirled away by a gale and then brought back by another
Adamant and rough   with no way to conceal

Its roundedness and fineness
Reticent   overlooked by the world
Yet unable to be possessed arbitrarily by anyone

The boulder on the mountain   which I must visit on Sundays
I often recall it
Realizing being busy all day and every day is merely
Bending the body and lifting the weight as light as a feather
Above one's head

Hymn to an Envoy

Under the branch-like lightning bolts and flares
He is trekking
While shouting and yelling
As slightly excited as an upcoming tempest

I comprehend this child
A travel-loving kid

Who has just brought back from afar a bouquet
In rainy and snowy weather earlier than spring
While striking out splashing sparks
As an apprentice at a blacksmith shop
He was composing hymns:

"Spring transports happiness between the sea and the clouds
In summer   the stamens and pistils of the stars
Have burned the entire firmament red
The gigantic celestial arc
Resembling the head of a sunflower is drooping
Just like Mother's belly   not only close to life
But also constituting life itself

A bird has flitted through a garden trying to awaken amid the rain
Skimmed between my arms and singing
And flown elsewhere with more hustle and bustle."

The branched lightning bolts and flashes
Are above the deep dense shades of summer
And in front of him

Oh the kid fond of attractive appearance and solo activities
I comprehend him

His once quietude and affability
Originate from the calming and abating of the gales of life
Indeed he wholeheartedly likes
Real gales
And even a blazing fire resounding through the zenith

At the moment   in the real unmanned region
With a face as clearly bright as that of an envoy
Either light or dark in the suburbs
Where thunder reverberates and lightning strikes
He will conceal all his pain in the tempest

Small Castle on the Border

Exile hither the czar showing up in dreams

A place where forefathers whipping horses to gallop speedily
Had the white bones of their foes and their own dissipate
Exile hither the desert   leas and damaged buckets

A place teeming with starshine as bitterly forlorn as jade's luster
And the wails and infectious diseases brought by a mother wolf
  called Juana
Exile hither the blizzards of language

And exile hither the moralists and didacts
As well as their powder mills

Spring or Blue

The full daylight is tormenting the moon in the sky
The empty blue of the celestial dome
Is excruciating a helicopter
My reticence and the colors of a toy crane
Highlight this spring   its bleakness and brilliance

Decadent yet nice   oh spring graduates
From light blue to dark blue and then to inky blue
Just like a hypothetical demise
The fate of a boy having taken off his mask is
He is being unrestrictedly dragged into the deep water
Of a lake abandoned by white swans last year

A deeper blue   a kind of spring continuously making
A tortured hum and buzz due to the frequent mating
Between the helicopter and the welkin
A fate containing both compassion and decadence
And belonging to the boy

Nevertheless I trust this boy and the pacification
Of his tempestuous body in the dark blue
And believe in the bewilderment he once had
After being forgotten by earthly slumbers
His tendency toward the inky blue means
He is most willing to be dragged down
And submerge himself in a truly dark lake
Where   like facing the grand finale
He aspires for the onset of the bright daylight

So as to ask for clean blue from the sky
More and denser than the mayflies
At the turn of spring and summer
Thriving sensually like a sudden outbreak of blue-green algae
And drooping hopelessly with a tendency to expire

Oh blue

Post Office

The pretty tasty fruit has all been moved to the balcony
And so have the berries forever dreamed of by an animal
Called goat from the depths of an old forest
Summer is here   so it doesn't matter
If they are higher   or more conspicuous

I only have a melancholy concrete balcony
That I might lose
Nevertheless the sun   water
And rebellious gales will come
And so will thunder   lightning and meteors
My restless friends are secretly discussing
Another party after the summer

My concrete balcony is at a high place
Whence I look down   all those keen on snatch
Those controlled by diseases and busyness
Those stirring up dust to sing with noise
Some are kin   others are foes
More are strangers
The balcony   fruits   summer
As well as our party
Are the things above their heads

As to how the fruits are joyfully consumed
And how the flock of people babble-gabble
And part in discord in the end   it doesn't matter
As it's only a friends' party

Only that a saying is very interesting:

"Post office   the heart of the world
We are letters sent out by someone
And being sent elsewhere in a hurry."

A Grove of Trees in the North

A wolf in the North is going to leave
Which is the business of a grove of trees
Something making the moon poignantly beautiful
And thought about by the wolf in its heart for long

The grove of trees   with interconnected roots
Has become one isolated tree after another
Ended up being the only one
After a wolf runs away from the North

(What a ridiculous tree   wobbling and tottering
In the sandstorm   as vehemently tormented
As the wolf's desire to leave)

The wolf in the North is running away
The last lone wolf   with hoary unkempt fur
As prostrate and overwhelmed as a rat in a year of famine
Leaving behind an expanse of desolate woods
As well as all the legendary greed and cunning
On its thin waist and skinny legs
Is cutting and running

The woods guarded by the only tree
Are left behind by the wolf   and so are
The livestock which from then on can only have a thin neck
And some aggrieved and crestfallen people
Who are neither hunters nor herders

The wolf in the North is escaping   of the woods left behind
Where wolves lived

The thirst for leaving   in the sandstorm
Between the skyline and the woods' hoary chinks
Is dispirited day by day

Alchemy

As an indomitable person
I have extracted many weeps and almost negligible agonies
From the inside of a massive frost-cracked boulder
After many years of twists and turns

As a quite mythologized person
While a careless gardener isn't paying attention
I have searched out a missing baby and the fragments of
A liar's skull broken from behind by a blunt object
In a tree controlled by iron and glass for ages
And its aggrievedly blooming blossoms

Actually my real identity is a narc
Proficient in alchemy
Having always been preparing for a trip to a distant land
To excavate mountains and blast rocks
I will be the one traveling around the world
More mysterious than the legends
In the martial arts world of ancient China
A master of all the arcana of alchemy

Spider

Snuggling in your soul is a spider
Whose shape
Is also the shape of your soul
The way the spider spins silk
Is how your soul looks
When it is unable to cut off ties
With a phantom

All of these are like fate
As if determined in a past life
The silhouette of the spider
Is also the silhouette of your soul
Wherever you go
It follows you

Too many times you bid adieu
On your face is too much melancholy
And haze-like befuddlement
You like to weave into the crowd
Attempting to let those prominent hunchbacks
And swollen noses help you rub something off
You have been looking for the place
Where many people leave and return alternately
And move constantly without settling down
To inquire about the whereabouts
Of some other spiders
This is because you haven't seen
Any hide or hair of a spider for long
Which is also the sign of your soul
That resurrects once every day
Or even of yourself

Fog and Yellow Leaves

In the dead of the night I looked at
The bizarre shape of the Astrology Museum
On a street called Nameless
With its dome locked by fog
And the trees lining both sides of the street
Divested of foliage
And piercing the body of the thick fog
With their stark naked boughs

A female sanitation worker in a yellow vest
Is engrossed with the sweeping of the dark-toned light
All over the street
And the last batch of yellow leaves
Pressed to the bottom of the light

The overcast sky   just like the ashen fog
Seems to snow   but with unspeakable concerns
Hesitates about whether or not it should snow

Empty Train

An empty train is traversing
The vast expanse of northern wilderness
Valleys shrouded in tenebrosity
And the bowels of clusters of peaks

On the empty train only with two passengers
In the absolutely empty North
A man and a woman
Remain indifferent while witnessing in person
A wild goat and a lynx running wild outside
Almost frightened to death by the headlights

On the empty train with hollow coaches
The two passengers having never met before
Of unknown origin and to an unknown destination
Have missed at the same time a roadside child
Waving his greetings   in the last village

The empty train   with completely blank light
Flashes by like a specter
Lighting up the face of the only child left in the North
Daring to stand in the tenebrosity

The two passengers stare vacantly ahead
And have missed   at the moment
When the darkness is illuminated
That child   and what's behind him
The spaciously empty North

Where Does the Narrative as Light as a Zephyr Come From

For having removed the plough from the land
He was cruelly flogged with thorns by his father on a mountain
On the mountain gently flitted by the glare of the scorching sun
Compared to the rocks burned black   Father's palms
Were more vicious and scheming
Before starting as a porcelain-firing master worker
He used to work as a raw brick maker
At a secret illegal brick factory
And then a coal-filling man in a machinery plant for a while
Adding coal to a colossal steel furnace
And controlling the duration and degree of heating
He once boiled down and dried nine rivers in the fire
Year in and year out
Only he knows the secret of the disappearance of the nine rivers

When nine giant dragons repeatedly appear in his dreams
And start to romp with nine phoenixes as well as with him
As the narrator   he has determined the way
To narrate about his father as well as about himself

A way as light as a zephyr
The way things disappear as simply as a puff of smoke does

North North

My hometown is in the North
My fairy-tale house is built right in the thirsty desert
Where the degree of cowardice of a flower
Is comparable to that of a lamp

My hometown is in the North
Where my fairy-tale house is kindhearted
Oh the pusillanimous lamp
And the flower facing an impasse
Are two little babies in my fairy-tale house

My fairy-tale house is kind
Without disfavoring the spaciously empty North
The lamp and the flower by the door
Are each other's umbra

My hometown is in the North
On the tip of the knife with which the north wind
Sweeps through the sand dunes
And in the innermost heart of a fairy tale
Filled with hidden pain

My hometown is in the North
I will ceaselessly tell my fairy tale to the North
In the hope that my North can slowly grow up
In my fairy tale

Stonemason

A stonemason was my father
Living in the North
Under the clearly bright yet sadly indignant starlight

He spent many nights on the cliffs—

In the dark he kept rolling boulders down the hill
Thus infuriating a great river
And the slumber of the people in the canyon

He spent a lot of daytime on a huge quarry—

The scorching sun silenced the air
He alone was chiseling one after another
Rough tough rocks arrayed in midsummer
Occasionally while carving the fine details with an iron chisel
He would also vociferate loudly with excitement
"Look! These rocks can eventually turn white
Not only white but also beautiful"

The stonemason oh my father
Had an unsociable and eccentric yet self-indulgent life which
Day after day after each sunset
Sank deeper and deeper in the gloom of dusk
And the carbon blackness of his body
Regardless of the sparks brighter than the starlight
Splashing under the sad and angry northern starshine
Unaware that in the darkness not far away
I often waited for him to return while intoning poetry

Oh why car lights   came and went in a hurry
Had just illuminated a large area of the deep serene canyon
And then left it heavily to the darkness

Man Chasing Massive Boulders

Massive boulders are avalanching from high above the world
From all corners of the world
With no need for high winds
No need for changing from one altitude to another
No need for terraces from high to low
Or the curvature of a bow or half-moon
Or the trajectory of a howitzer or spacecraft
And rumbling over from all the details of the world

The man chasing the rumbling rolling boulders from behind
Being chased by even larger boulders from his back
Racing ceaselessly while yelling and shouting
Constantly leaping up due to overexcitement
Repeatedly missing the strikes of the chasing boulders
Hence turning indifferent toward danger
Is a happy man with the overwhelming innocence of a child
And the mettle of a ferocious beast
To dedicate itself to the world in defiance of all consequences

The world is at the center of terra firma of the ocean
Of the emptiness inside a balloon yet to burst
The massive boulders are rolling down toward the world's center
The man chasing the colossal boulders at the center of the world
Seems to be playing an unexpected yet well controllable game

Chasing the massive boulders
While being chased by them

A Way to Clean Up Nightmares and Life

You must take with you a broom fair and square
Pretending it is only a moon-shaped fan
Forge deeper ahead step-by-step in the depths of life
And experience what seem to be seen in your dreams
The nearly crumbled life and body
And the plastic female mannequins
Next to the door of a fashion shop   torn apart
Apparently with a bit of debauchery   stark naked
If you run into an old woman selling flowers
Stopping you and swaying a bunch of flowers
Or see petals scattered all over the ground just after she has left
You must keep cool   pretend to be deeply perplexed
And accidentally entangled with yourself
And then quickly flash by
Or let another hapless guy zoom there
If afterward you seem to end up in bad luck
By inadvertently encountering dump trucks
Dashing toward you as if fleeing
Spilling along the road debris of unknown origin
Harder to deal with and thus more treacherous than shattered glass
Thereby suddenly increasing the difficulty of cleaning
Then you must stop and hunker down to clean them up
As to whether this road is your way back
Or the way you will have to pass when you go out soon
And whether this road is for humans   worms   or even ghosts
They are no longer your concerns
What is more important is   you must hunker down
To clean them up

As if cleaning a nightmare with venomous stingers
Or a road where an old friend has peacefully fallen into slumber
Or a road on which a swan looks for spring   or a person
As pure as a swan   stretches out his wings hidden for a lifetime
And then flies gracefully and leisurely toward heaven

Rock Arrangement

I beheld a man arranging rocks
Engrossed in solitude amidst a mound of them
With his back to the others
Yelling at the rocks alone all day and every day
With a deafening harsh voice
Just like a rooster

The rocks were mined from the mountains
Transported from the quarry piece by piece
They also must be so arranged
And have the regular yet candid rhythms attributed to rocks
Manifested loudly and gracefully
So as to cover up the traits of cuts left by irons

The one looking stumpy due to a slight hunchback
Was a man arranging rocks with heart and soul
Again and again he caressed
The wounded rocks well-arranged after killings
I even witnessed in person how he scrutinized his shadow
Against the wall of stacked massive rocks
With his visage so focused and content
As if he had unexpectedly encountered a long-lost old friend

I beheld the man arranging the rocks
Seemingly somewhat cold at first glance
Making unusual noises with things
But content with taciturnity just like an inmate
Stacking up the rocks piece by piece
With the magnificent tempo as of a symphony
With the perseverant temperament and exquisite texture

Of the rocks

The man arranging the rocks I beheld
I would rather believe you saw too
And even have confidence that once upon a time
You were the man arranging the rocks
You are the very man arranging the rocks

ACKNOWLEDGMENTS

The author and translators would like to thank the editors of the following publications in which portions of this work previously appeared:

AzonaL: "A Coordinator's Canyon," "Northern Writer," "Those Northern Blue Lakes," and "Sleeping with a Mirror"

The Common: "Photo of Free Life in the E-Era" in its China folio

The Dead Mule School of Southern Literature: "Story of Searching for Spring in the Suburbs," "Hymn to an Envoy," and "Post Office"

Defunct Magazine: "Legendary Bad Girl" and "Legend of Xi'an"

Delos: A Journal of Translation and World Literature: "The Extremity of the Earth," "A Man Is Leaving the North," "Man Studying His Own Shadow," "Eulogy to the Qin Mountains," and "Settling"

The Dodge: "The Beauty of Killing" and "Melancholy"

DoubleSpeak: "Onlooker" and "Sleeping with a Mirror"

Exchanges: Journal of Literary Translation: "South   North," "Balloon and Emptiness," "I Have Captured Another Monster," and "Horse"

Firmament: "Doll with a Straw Headscarf," "Lurkers' Portrait," "Man in a Black Bear Skin," "Tiger," and "Stranded"

Flyway: Journal of Writing & Environment: "Territory" and "Empty Train"

The Fourth River: "Fog and Yellow Leaves"

Heavy Feather Review: "Plane Descending in Raging Mist and Snow," "Flight," "Snow's Language Awakens in the Tenebrosity," "At the Back of All Things," and "North   North"

Hedge Apple: "Coffee-Hawking Outlander" and "Stranger Comes to Visit in a Strange Way"

The Hopkins Review: "Black Iron and Dark Cloud"

IHRAF Literary: "Where Does the Narrative as Light as a Zephyr Come From"

The Ilanot Review: "How Did Four Dung Beetles Easily Take Away Earth" and "Yatter-Natter About Poetry and Biology"

Interim: "Tunnel Warfare," "Whales," "Night Train," and "Place I Passed by Occasionally"

International Poetry Review: "Imagining the Life of a Spider in a Village," "Elaborating on the Boulders on Mount Hua," and "Outlanders"

Kyoto Journal: "The Qin Mountains: The Seven States of the Boulder Manor" and "Seven Days in the Qin Mountains"

Life and Legends: "Mu Us Desert, Encountering a Herder Too Old to Have Consciousness" and "A Way to Clean Up Nightmares and Life"

The Momentist: "Over-Blustery Gale," "Lone River," and "After Abrupt Disappearance of a Lake"

NonBinary Review: "Calamity of Pearls"

Notre Dame Review: "Encounter with an Enigmatic Fish" and "Legendary Red of the Qin Mountains"

Oxford Anthology of Translation: "The Place I Want to Go"

Packingtown Review: "How to Transform into an Urbanite" and "Spring or Blue"

Penn Journal of Arts and Sciences: "Hometown and Pearl" and "Mary Suite No. 1"

The Poet: "A Story of Return to Home Village"

Poetry Northwest: "Discovery by a Mirror Image Researcher"

Red Rock Review: "Snow-Chasing Girl," "Girl Coerced into a Snowy Night and Its Vacancy by a Dream," "Mirror," and "Spider"

RHINO Poetry: "Rock Arrangement"

SAND: "Rivulet of Occasionality"

Tilted House: "Doll with a Straw Headscarf"

Tab Journal: "Tenebrosity" and "Situations of a Bird and Two People"

West Branch: "Nocturnal Singer," "Mountain in My Childhood," and "Reticent Man"

Winning Writers: "A Man Is Leaving the North"

The Poet reprinted the poem "How Did Four Dung Beetles Easily Take Away Earth" in the *Our Changing Earth* anthology.

A set of five poems, "Plane Descending in Raging Mist and Snow," "Flight," "Snow's Language Awakens in the Tenebrosity," "At the Back of All Things," and "North North," was the winner of the 2021 *Zachary Doss Friends in Letters Memorial Fellowship* organized by *Heavy Feather Review*. We are grateful to the 2021 *John Dryden Translation Competition* for longlisting the set of poems titled

The World's Ten Portraits which includes "How to Transform into an Urbanite," "Coffee-Hawking Outlander," "Discovery by a Mirror Image Researcher," "Wild Kid," "Fog and Yellow Leaves," "Escaper in a Heavy Snow," "Hymn to an Envoy," "Spring or Blue," "Stranger Comes to Visit in a Strange Way," and "Post Office." Also, many thanks to the 2022 *John Dryden Translation Competition* for longlisting the set of poems titled *Imaginary World* which includes "Imagining the Life of a Spider in a Village," "Encounter with an Enigmatic Fish," "Spider Is Leaving the Place You Are Leaving," "Fish-Shaped Snow," "Excavator," "Story of Tree Planting," "Story of Searching for Boulders on the North Mountains," "Legendary Red of the Qin Mountains," and "A Nonexistent Mountain."

"Black Iron and Dark Cloud" was nominated by *The Hopkins Review* for the *Best Literary Translations 2024* anthology published by Deep Vellum in 2024. "Rock Arrangement" was nominated by *RHINO Poetry* for the *Best Literary Translations 2025* anthology also published by Deep Vellum in 2025. "How Did Four Dung Beetles Easily Take Away Earth" was nominated by *The Ilanot Review* for the *2024 Best of the Net Anthology.* "Situations of a Bird and Two People" was nominated by *Tab Journal* for the *2025 Best of the Net Anthology.* "Stranger Comes to Visit in a Strange Way" was nominated by *Hedge Apple* for the *2025 Best of the Net Anthology.*

Onlooker, a twenty-two-poem chapbook, was a finalist for the *Toad Press International Chapbook Series* in 2024. Nineteen poems of the chapbook are from *Rock Arrangement.* A set of twelve poems from this poetry collection won the *Toad Press International Chapbook Series* in January 2025 and was published by Toad Press as a chapbook titled *Middle-Aged Man's Self-Portrait* in July 2025 in the United States. The poems are: "Mu Us Desert, Encountering a Herder Too Old to Have Consciousness," "A Man Is Leaving the North," "Doll with a Straw Headscarf," "Tunnel Warfare," "Man in a Black Bear Skin," "Coffee-Hawking Outlander," "How to Transform into an Urbanite," "Man Studying His Own Shadow," "I Have Captured Another Monster," "Stranger Comes to Visit in a Strange Way," "Calamity of Pearls," and "Middle-Aged Man's Self-Portrait."